EVERY CAST

EVERY CAST

CHRONICLES OF A DEEPLY HOOKED ANGLER

STEPHEN SAUTNER

ILLUSTRATIONS BY DAVE TAFT

LP

LYONS
PRESS

Essex, Connecticut

LP
LYONS PRESS

An imprint of The Globe Pequot Publishing Group, Inc.
64 South Main Street
Essex, CT 06426
www.globepequot.com

British Library Cataloguing in Publication Information available

Library of Congress Cataloging-in-Publication Data available

ISBN 9781493092321 (cloth) | ISBN 9781493092338 (epub)

*To my non-fishing parents who gave me a rod and reel when
I turned sixteen and unknowingly unleashed the madness.
The message on my birthday card should have read:
"The first cast is free."*

*And to my wife and son who
continue to enable my habit, thank you and don't wait up.*

CONTENTS

PART VII: WITH ROD TUBE IN HAND

PART VIII: FINAL CASTS

Introduction

Every Cast

THEY ARE OUT THERE, RIGHT NOW, FISHING AMONG US, CASTING in plain view. You may have waded downstream of one just yesterday or walked past another at a boat launch or back bay last week. At first glance, they appear normal. Most are middle-aged or approaching it, but some are older and a few younger. All have faces furrowed from hard miles spent in sun and wind, or from sleepless nights chasing a late tide or an after-dark spinner fall. Some of them may appear a bit disheveled, almost like they've been drinking, yet they cast soberly with a clarity of purpose. Some smoke—either tobacco, or nowadays cannabis—and a bluish haze sometimes surrounds them mid-stream. Still others resemble wiry athletes, wolfing down energy bars and guzzling electrolyte-infused water—whatever it takes for maximum performance.

Things start to get weird when you approach one at an angler's parking lot or along a fishing trail and ask a casual: "Anything happening?" Initially, they may mutter a one-word answer or ignore you altogether. But ask another leading question, something like "Is it me, or do Hendricksons seem off this year?" or "You think yellow is still the best color for stripers?" and watch the dam start to crack, then burst. What follows is a tsunami of rapid-fire opinions about bugs, baitfish, wind direction, barometric pressure, cubic feet per second, tides, or rod tapers. Ask those same questions when fish are active, and they become twitchy, unable to complete sentences as they look through you, calculating their next cast.

For these are the fish junkies—angling's version of meth heads. Weirdos forever chasing the dopamine jolt that comes from the perfect presentation, the perfect rise, the perfect release. The perfect.

I know because I am one of them.

For more than four and a half decades, ever since my parents bought me a rod in a blister pack for my sixteenth birthday in 1980, along with a how-to book called *The ABCs of Fishing*, I have been hopelessly ensnared in a bird's nest of fly line, tippet, mono, braid, and shock leaders. Riffles gurgle through my brain. Tides flood my psyche. When I'm not on or in the water, my days are spent thinking about the next hatch or the waxing moon. I pantomime double hauls while walking to the bathroom. I drift off to sleep thinking of rising trout or busting stripers. I sometimes jar myself awake with a hook set or broken line.

Over the years, my family has learned to tolerate this. They watch with bemusement as I endlessly gather and sort my tackle like some harmless man-child poring over his collection of Pokémon cards. They know that the night before any fishing trip, I will toss and turn like an eight-year-old on Christmas Eve. When I return from a particularly satisfying day (or night) and declare that "my tank is full!" they politely nod and know that, within twenty-four hours, the twitching will resume. When it does, I fill my car with gear and once more head afield. Fishing trip after fishing trip.

Freshwater. Saltwater. River. Stream. Lake. Surf. Ice.

Fly. Spinning. Graphite. Glass. Bamboo.

Winter. Spring. Summer. Fall.

Sometimes I board airplanes with rod tubes strapped to my back, carry-ons stuffed with tackle, heading to some far-flung place. All for fish. Every. Cast.

And yes, it is fish I seek, but other things, too: the earthy smell of rivers or the tang of brine, green woodlands dripping with songbirds, a breaching whale, the rhythmic onrush and receding of a black surf on a moonless night. Elemental things that my body forever craves, things that I can't live without.

And with that, I declare with neither pride nor shame, but as my simple, unvarnished truth: *Hi, my name is Stephen, and I am a fishing addict.*

My testimonial, gathered from stories compiled over these past several decades, follows.

PART I
SWEET

It's all you ever think about!

—UNNAMED GIRLFRIEND, 1985

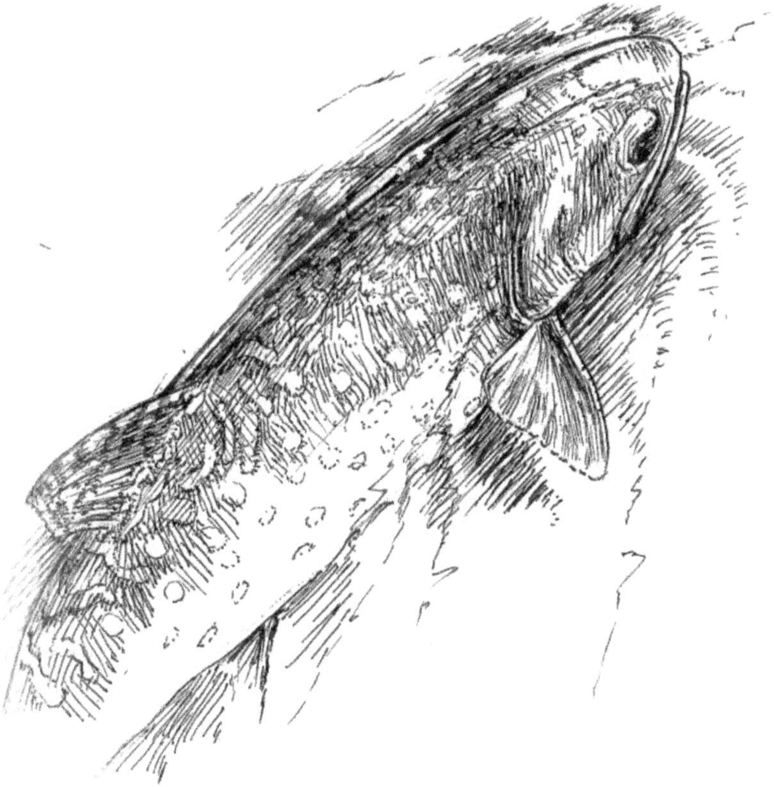

CARPE MAY 12TH

SOME DAYS YOU SHOULD JUST TAKE THE DAY OFF. LAST MAY 12th was one of those days.

If I had not—if I had let May 12th slip away and it had become just another workday where I woke up, fought traffic, sat in meetings, and answered emails and phone calls; then fought some more traffic, got home, ate dinner, watched TV, and went to bed—well, let's just say it would have been a mistake.

But I did take May 12th off, clearing my calendar and posting an out-of-office message—especially when I saw an approaching high-pressure system settling in and temperatures rising into the low seventies.

As Morgan Freeman said in *The Shawshank Redemption*, "May is one damn fine month to be working outdoors." The same can be said of fishing—particularly here in the Northeast, where options can overflow like a banquet. Where I live in New Jersey, stripers are hot on the tails of arriving schools of menhaden, while bluefish have invaded shallow bays ready to blast anything that chugs, pops, or skips their way.

But it was the call of freshwater streams and rivers that had me loading the car the night before. Mayfly hatches neared their seasonal peak on local trout waters, while American shad were reaching pre-spawn critical mass in the Delaware River.

I planned for a long day, packing the car with two fly rods, two spinning rods, assorted tackle bags, fly boxes, and waders along with a cooler packed with a sandwich, snacks, and water. I told my wife not to expect me for dinner then hit the road at 9:00 a.m. after most of the local rush hour subsided. Yes, it was fun driving past people headed for work.

My first stop was a small stream that tumbled past a state road. This was the harvest part of the trip, and my quarry was stocked trout that hopefully would wind up in my smoker. I treat this particular stream like a prized thicket of blackberries. I'll hit once or twice a season, load up, and return again next year.

I pulled into a dirt turnout, grabbed my ultralight, tackle bag number 1 and canvas creel. No fly rod or waders here; this would be a quick drive-by. A fifty-foot walk down a funky trail led to the stream. Even though the road is only yards away, once I reached the first pool, I entered a little world unto itself. The sound of rushing water, punctuated by a few scattered songbirds calling—yellow warblers, waterthrushes, and vireos—replaced the noise of traffic. A green canopy shaded the stream and blocked the highway. And it smelled like spring in there—earthy and dewy and peppered with new growth.

The pool was just how I had hoped: clear and flowing and with a dozen stockers holding at the tailout. And, true to form, they grabbed or at least followed my spinner on nearly every cast. A limit could have come easily from here if that's what I wanted, but I chose instead to creel just three rainbows and leave the rest for others. I quickly cleaned the fish streamside and left. After a stop at a nearby convenience store for a bag of ice, I continued westward where more water beckoned.

At noontime, I stood in a grassy parking area along the Delaware River eating lunch and leaning against my car with the hatchback up. I had already rigged my seven-weight, and my stripping basket and waders stood at the ready. A yellow-billed cuckoo called above me while various warblers sang in an adjacent thicket. The sun felt good on my face. Two cars were already parked there, but I felt no need to rush on this leisurely day. When I eventually made my way to the river, I spotted three retired guys standing knee-deep thirty feet apart. All of them fly-fished, hooking shad on every third or fourth cast. I walked a hundred yards upstream, waded out, and stripped running line into the basket. Then I roll cast the shooting head past the rod tip, hauled once, and watched the chartreuse shad fly shoot out and touch down on the edge of the current. I let it settle for a few seconds before stripping it back with sharp pulls.

Halfway in, a fish bumped the fly but missed. On my next cast, something took solidly. It turned out to be a good-sized buck shad that jumped twice and took some line before a quick release. The next fish stayed deep and turned out to be a large roe—probably five pounds and as deep as my outstretched hand. A few casts later, I caught its twin sister. Back they went, too, along with another buck. Mixed in with the landed fish were various bumps and missed hits. Around two o'clock the wind began picking up, and I decided to walk back to my car and swap the seven-weight for an eight-foot light spinning rod. But despite another half hour of casting, I couldn't get another hit. Meanwhile the retired guys continued to pick at shad with their fly rods. One guy was clearly in the zone more than his buddies and probably landed at least a dozen. On another day, this might have made me slightly jealous. But on this day, May 12th, I was genuinely happy for him. You see, I had plenty more fishing left to do and more water to visit.

I walked back to the car and stowed my tackle before eating an apple and drinking some water. It was time for my next stop—a wild trout stream that flows into the Delaware from the Pennsylvania side of the river.

A half hour later, I parked along a quiet wooded road. I put on my vest and grabbed my five-weight. After a ten-minute walk, I reached the river, which looked perfect: clear and with a good head of water thanks to rains earlier in the week. I skipped the first large pool and headed upstream to reach my favorite spot on the creek—a long run that starts out swiftly then slows gradually—but never too slow—as it deepens. Lots of submerged boulders and grottos make it look like a place to hook a truly large trout.

With a warm sun and blue skies, it was still too early to expect to see much by way of hatching bugs and rising fish, so I decided to try a nymph under an indicator. I am no fan of this technique, but it still beats sitting on the bank waiting for something to happen.

On my very first drift—more just to pay out a little more line from the reel—I saw the indicator jerk under. I lifted, thinking the fly hung on a boulder. Instead, a massive football of a brown trout greyhounded out of the water and threw the fly. Holy crap—what a fish! Could have been twenty inches or larger. Wish I had gotten more than a half-second glimpse. But despite my best subsequent drifts with the nymph, followed by a streamer, then a big attractor dry, I could not buy another strike.

I decided to rest the spot and sat on a large streamside boulder. The sounds of running water, combined with the sweet calls of more warblers, bubbling catbirds, and thrushes, entertained my ears. I may have dozed off for a few minutes.

Then, splash—a fish rose maybe thirty feet downstream of me. I waited and it rose again. I couldn't see any bugs on the water except for a few black caddis buzzing around. Another rise. I decided to try a Hendrickson. Even though the annual hatch was long over, I figured the trout would still recognize it as food. It did; it crashed the fly on the first drift, flashing pink and silver, before tearing off downstream. A nice rainbow.

The trout stopped, then held in heavy water for what felt like a long time before tearing off more line. Though it never jumped, it did an admirable job of beating me up as best it could. Finally it yielded to rod pressure and turned on its side where I slid it toward me. It was a lovely wild fish, sixteen inches long and thick. It had an electric steelhead-like blush on its cheeks, a brilliant pink stripe running down muscular flanks, and flashes of white on the tips of its fins. I twisted the fly free and held the fish in the current for another moment before letting it go.

I basked in a fishy afterglow for a while, but then a long time went by with virtually no action. A couple of fish rose just once, and before I knew it, it was well after six o'clock when I decided enough was enough and headed for my car.

When I got there, two other anglers had parked next to me, and were about to fish a series of pools just downstream from the road. Sweaty and spent, I began taking off my waders. I chatted with one of the guys who was just finishing rigging up his fly rod. He told me the fishing had been very good the night before and that it was a late bite with sulfurs hatching just around dark.

Then he headed down a trail, leaving me wondering what to do. On any other day, I may have said "next time," thrown my gear in the car, and driven home. But by God, this was May 12th. I had taken the day off to fish, and fish I will until the day is done. And it was not.

I rolled my waders back up, wolfed down a granola bar, and guzzled the last of my water. I clipped my headlamp to my hat just in case, and back to the creek I headed. Ten minutes later, I found myself at the first pool I had initially skipped. Now the creek looked even fishier in the soft evening light. And as if on cue, a trout rose once, then twice.

I stuck with the Hendrickson and cast it to a narrow bubble line directly across from me. The fish came up in a confident rise that turned out to be an even larger rainbow at seventeen and a half inches and just as beautiful as the first. Then a few minutes ticked by with no more rises, so I walked to the run upriver to see if anything was coming up there. A few catbirds worked above the stream, periodically flying out and delicately grabbing mayflies on the wing.

But no rises, so I sat on the same boulder and waited again. Then a few minutes later, a fish rose below me. It came up a second time. I began casting to it, straining to watch the fly track through the current in the silvery glare made from the evening light. I made another cast. The fly drifted a few yards before the trout slashed at it violently but somehow missed. I waited a minute before casting again hoping it would forget what had just happened. This time, the fish took the fly hard, throwing water. I set the hook and felt the deep, satisfying weight of a very nice trout hooked in swift water. It took line in one long and powerful surge, and for a second, I thought it would blow out of the pool. It stopped and sulked in deep water for a few moments, then swam toward me before screaming out a bunch of line for a second time. Eventually it swam into slower water and allowed me to bring it closer, closer still, and then finally into my hand.

Another fine, solid, wild fish—an eighteen-inch brown trout with blue cheeks and scattered, dark, no-nonsense spotting. I released it and was now absolutely ready to leave. Though it was still well before dark and the upcoming sulfur hatch, I had finally gotten my fill and was ready to shed my waders, stow my tackle, and head home. And I did, but not before a fine fishermen's feast served at the nearest drive-thru. At ten o'clock, some eleven hours, 120 round-trip miles, and three streams later, I walked through my front door tired, stiff, sunburned, and deeply satisfied.

So, to my fellow anglers, my advice to you is this: take that day off. Don't let the next May 12th slip away.

Gone Trout Fishing
with Some Clown

WHILE TROUT FISHING ON A RURAL PENNSYLVANIA SPRING
creek a few summers ago, I came upon a five-foot-tall wooden
clown standing in the river. Cut from a piece of plywood, and
painted in simple shades of red, yellow, and blue, it must have
come from one of the small towns a few miles upstream.

I pictured it washing down from an annual fireman's fair
or Fourth of July carnival during a heavy downpour. Or maybe
some kids, bored with summer vacation, stole it, then heaved it
off a bridge and ran. In any case, now the clown stood smiling,
wedged in a logjam, with its bright polka-dot trousers and string
of deflated balloons.

But the clown also marked a favorite pool, one where fourteen-
and fifteen-inch brown trout would rise in the afternoon to
hatching mayflies. That summer, with the river empty of springtime anglers, I fished with the clown as my only company.

When I landed a particularly nice trout, I would show the
clown before I released it. If I missed a good rise, or piled a cast
up in an overhanging branch, I would glance across the pool at the
clown and chuckle. Week after week it was always there, happily
smiling, eyes shut as if basking in the summer sun.

One day, late in the season, the trout rose well into the evening to a hatch of tiny blue-winged olives. Before I knew it, a misty evening gloom rapidly swallowed up the forest around me, and I could barely see my line on the water.

I was thinking about changing to a larger fly that I could see better when a sudden, uneasy feeling came over me.

I stood still for a moment, listening to the water gurgle around me. Then, slowly, I turned and looked at the clown.

By now, after weeks in the river, its colors had bleached to a ghostly pale, and long tendrils of green algae grew from its submerged clown feet. The once bright smile and closed eyes had faded into lifeless slits. A floating log or branch had knocked it off-center, and it leaned to one side like an old, settled gravestone.

A chill shot through my body, and I found myself wading to the bank as fast as I could. The river tugged and pulled at my waders as I splashed along crazily, spooking every fish in the pool. When my fly snagged in the brush along the shore, I snapped it off without stopping, and half-ran up the trail to my truck a half mile away. Forty-five minutes later, driving sixty-five miles per hour on the Pennsylvania Turnpike, I felt a little better.

A week later, a two-day autumn rainstorm sent the river raging over its banks. When I returned, the clown had long since washed away, replaced by what looked like an old shopping cart—from upstream, I guess.

WHEN THINGS GO RIGHT

As anglers, we all know that fishing truisms like leaky waders, wind knots, and blown hook sets can gnaw at us between casts. But sometimes, a yang of brilliant light shines down to counteract yin's dark energy.

Last January at the Edison Fly Fishing Show, I found myself wandering past the booth of a local Trout Unlimited (TU) chapter where an enthusiastic volunteer was giving the hard sell to buy raffle tickets. We made just enough eye contact for me to get entangled in his web.

"C'mon! Buy a ticket!" he said.

I only had a twenty-dollar bill, and tickets were five bucks each, so he made damn sure I bought four. I wrote down my name and phone number on each ticket while he told me about the prize, which was some sort of rod. To tell you the truth, I was only half-paying attention since no one ever seems to win raffles, especially me. Then he mentioned the drawing would take place later in the spring and wished me good luck. By the time I got home, I had already forgotten all about it.

But then in mid-June, I received a call from the chapter president who informed me that I had in fact won the raffle. Cool; now what was the prize again? Turns out I had scored a top-of-the-line nine-foot five-weight from one of the elite rod makers. A quick search online showed a retail price that sent my jaw into my coffee. The president asked if I could pick the rod up that evening. Why yes, yes, I could.

A few days later, I stood knee-deep on a favorite Catskill trout river holding my shiny new rod. Recent rains had recharged the stream with a good head of water. It was still early in the day; no bugs yet, but friends reported that both golden stones and slate drakes were hatching. Maybe I could raise a fish on an attractor in some fast water.

I chose a PhD, a whimsical attractor pattern by British fly tier and friend Nigel Nunn. The fly is a buggy amalgam of deer hair and grizzly hackle, with a spun and clipped head like a shaggy muddler. It's tied on a small hook that stays tucked in its hackles and allows for unfettered natural movement—often the key to getting a fish to take when nothing is showing.

I made a few casts with the new rod and could tell right away I had won a Ferrari. Or maybe it was a Lamborghini. Whichever the case, it may have been the smoothest rod I had ever cast, like a bionic boron/graphite extension of my right arm. A small trout interrupted my casting bliss slashing at the fly but missing. As is often the case with attractors and showy rises, the fish refused to come back for a second look.

I eased a little farther into the flow, false casting while eyeballing a dark slot on the far side of a fast run. Foamy water eddied just enough to reveal a possible holding spot for a nicer fish. The fly dropped at the slot's far end. I checked the rod high dancing the PhD like a big stonefly laying its eggs. It made it less than a foot. The take was emphatic; a big brown porpoised showing a thick back before taking the fly down, hooking itself.

The trout shook its head just below the surface revealing its full bulk. I gasped and found myself saying out loud just one word: "*Big*." I held the new rod low like I was fighting a tarpon, trying to use its full power to convince the fish not to blow out of the slot. Just downstream, a brawling riffle loomed ready to swallow up the trout, fly, and leader, not to mention my dreams. For what felt like a long time, neither of us yielded, stubborn as two river boulders. But then the fish moved a few yards downstream to where the slot began to reorganize into faster water. I kept the rod even lower now as the brown repeatedly tried to surge away from me. After another tense minute, I felt that bittersweet moment when you break a fish's spirit, and it is now yours to lose. I backed into slower water easing it closer and closer. Instead of trying to fit the trout into my net, I coaxed it into the shallows where it lay on its side just long enough to allow me to take a single image before backing out the fly. By the time I put away my phone, the big brown had already powered back into the run and vanished. Later, holding a tape measure against the rod, I gave the trout twenty inches—maybe twenty-one.

Standing there on the side of the river after the release, I had that rarest of all feelings of not needing to make another cast—at least for the moment. The river chuckled past. In the foliage behind me, an oriole, indigo bunting, and scarlet tanager traded songs debating who was the prettiest. I held this gleaming new rod that had just caught its first-ever fish and wondered what I did to deserve all of this. Maybe it was like winning the raffle itself—just random luck. Sometimes in angling, things don't need further explanation.

Alone on a Catskill Headwater

Less than two miles from where I stand in this six-foot-wide tributary flows its eminence, the Upper Delaware River, with its steroidal wild browns and 'bows, banquet halls of insect hatches, and all the associated glory that goes with them.

Yet I am here, calf-deep, in wading sandals, shorts, and a T-shirt, casting a toy-sized one-ounce two-weight for native brookies and scale-model yearling rainbows. Cold water purls around my bare legs. Green walls of spring growth shield me from the outside world.

A world away are the Delaware's ubiquitous drift boats and breathable, hi-modulus wade-fishers. Here, my only companions are creatures born in these woods and waters. Above, warblers, tanagers, and vireos flit, sing, and forage. If I decide to flip a streamside rock (and why not?), I may see the pinkish orange of a spring salamander clambering away. Pickerel frogs and American toads consider me from their hidden grottos as I quietly sidestep around them.

I make a cast—all ten feet of it—dropping a caddis into a chute of water that hurries around a wheelbarrow-sized rock. From a shadow, a trout rises up and takes the fly down. I lift, and the fish darts and jabs before skipping across a tongue of current toward my waiting hand.

I hold a rainbow maybe seven inches long, finely spotted and still wearing its parr marks. A wild trout born in this tributary. This will be its last spring here; it will soon head downstream and hit the weight room of the Big River and all-you-can-eat drakes, caddis, and golden stones.

I wade up to the next run. Here, I will need to make a side-cast beneath a branch to sneak the fly into a bubble line maybe three inches wide. If the Delaware is Pebble Beach, where booming eighty-foot double hauls get you to the cup, this stream is minigolf. The caddis touches down, and a brook trout stylishly leaps from the water and lands on top of it, hooking itself. But the show ends there; the epilogue is just a few head shakes and bores for the bottom. A six-inch male, with a longish snout and hand-painted red spots, stares at me while I back the drowned caddis from its lower jaw. Unlike the rolling-stone rainbow, the homebody brookie will remain in these friendly confines for its entire life, bound by its need for always-cold, spring-fed flows.

This six-foot-wide stream is my home water both figuratively and literally. I have owned a simple cabin on its banks since the early 2000s and have come to know it more intimately than any place I have ever fished. I have seen it through historic floods and crippling droughts, and I've watched its wild trout population ebb and flow. Each fish, whether I release it or simply watch it rise and miss, is as familiar to me as an old fishing chum.

I continue casting but start to think about the unfinished beer I left sweating on the porch just before I grabbed the two-weight on a whim. Might be time to finish it. So I head back to the cabin. I peel off my wading sandals and sit barefoot on the '70s couch that the previous owners left behind. The beer slides down easily. And it's still cold.

I watch the stream from the comfort of the porch. Maybe later this evening, I'll hit the Delaware. Yes, after dinner I will gear up and drive down to a turnoff and look for a spinner fall. Just then, I see the wink of a rise not ten yards from where I sit. I look closer and can see a few tan caddis now bouncing off the stream. The trout rises again.

I finish my beer and grab the two-weight. For now, the twenty-inchers can wait. But clearly these six-inchers cannot.

TRASH-TALKING TROUT

IN MUCH OF THE RURAL UNITED STATES, THE TOWN DUMP remains the great equalizer. Sometimes known as the more sanitary sounding "transfer station," it's the one place that virtually everyone has to visit, whether poor, well-off, or otherwise. It's where the lawyer, plumber, and grandmother comingle like aluminum, glass, and plastic. They stand side by side and heave bags of trash while catching up on high school sports, the weather, or maybe some local gossip.

For years, my own visits to the local transfer station have been brief and largely silent. Even though I have owned a second home in this Upper Delaware River community for more than two decades, I still feel like an outsider whenever I drive up. Maybe it's my out-of-state plates. So, while some visitors to the dump might linger and socialize, my routine is to toss my garbage in the hydraulic compactor as fast as I can, drop my mixed recyclables down a little chute that empties into a dumpster, and head out. It usually takes me a minute, maybe two. The only exception happened a few years ago, when I showed up with my old nineteen-foot fiberglass canoe lashed to the roof of my car. An enormous dead ash fell on it during the offseason when it was stored in my backyard, crushing the hull. Disposal involved a quick conversation with the station manager who, with a nod of his chin, directed me to the container reserved for household appliances. My dead boat found its final resting place among old washing machines and refrigerators.

So, I was surprised one recent Saturday when in the middle of chucking a few garbage bags into the hydraulic compactor, I heard someone call over to me: "Nice car!" I looked over and saw a guy around my age standing next to an identical late model Subaru. It wasn't like we were both driving matching DeLoreans, so I just waved. But then I saw the same National Park Service fishing permit I had on my bumper and realized I had stumbled into a fellow angler. So, we stood there among bulk containers and dumpsters and began to chat.

Turns out his place is in the village; mine's a few miles outside of town. He spends most of his time up here trout fishing. Me, too. Then he offered this: "The river is on fire right now. Slate drakes and olives. Big fish coming up in the riffles. Starts around three o'clock. My son got a twenty-inch rainbow yesterday."

This was good dope. I hadn't actually been up to my place in a couple of weeks and didn't realize the action had already transitioned into an early fall pattern with bugs and trout more active in the afternoon than evening. I thanked him for the tip and, before driving off, gave him the standard: "See you on the river." Or maybe I'd see him back at the dump. Whatever the case, I briefly felt like a local.

That afternoon, I hiked down a trail that wound through a forest of yellowing knotweed. I emerged in front of a series of runs punctuated by short rushing riffles. Beyond the river, a steep forested hillside rose up revealing some maples already haloed in gold. The first hour of casting turned out to be quiet, but by around 3:30, as promised, I began to see small olives catching in the afternoon light, along with a few lumbering slate drakes. Soon after that, heads began poking up in the flow, some throwing water or slurping audibly.

These trout were no pushovers, I quickly learned. I missed a few, including two slow-motion risers with thick backs that made me wince when I whiffed. But most ignored my flies altogether. Eventually I got lucky and connected with a decent rainbow that did its best imitation of a steelhead jumping all over the river. Then I bounced a good-sized brown. And to that one fish that came up steadily no more than twenty feet away taking a hundred of my best pitches, I say this: good eye. By 5:30, the bugs became scarce and the rises sporadic, so I reeled up and left. A half hour later, I sat on the porch of my cabin sipping a beer and thinking about my next visit to the transfer station, which, as it turns out, is an excellent place for the juiciest kind of gossip.

River of Sinners

I KNEW . . .

I knew the Magalloway in western Maine was considered the second-best river in the United States for big wild brook trout. I read the stories and watched YouTube videos of anglers landing eighteen-, nineteen-, and twenty-inchers. Deep, thick, thrashing fish that looked more like heavy Arctic char from Alaska than dainty "brookies."

I also knew the Magalloway was big water. WWE body-slamming water. I studied topo maps and marveled how a river could lose elevation so quickly without a major waterfall. This was a river for carbide cleats, a wading staff, and maybe a life jacket. The kind of water where you keep your wallet in a Ziploc bag so the authorities can identify the body.

And I knew that my friend John Waldman lost his Personal Best brook trout here. He described how an immense dark shape rose off the bottom and sucked down his dry followed by ponderous headshakes and the heartbreak of a pulled hook.

Yes, I knew all these things. And still I insisted on fishing with 6x tippet.

I followed a trail to the Magalloway, my jaunty ten-foot Euronymphing rod bouncing in my hand, confident as I could be on new water. It was late July, well past peak hatch time, but the river still ran cool from the bottom release of nearby Aziscohos Dam.

My plan was to run a tandem of tungsten Frenchies through every fishable pocket and slot. I honed this technique on fast-water streams in the Catskills. Fifteen feet of soft mono, three feet of sighter, four more feet of 6x tippet. It destroys. One afternoon last spring, I hooked so many trout that a buddy fishing dries in the same run asked me to please stop.

The night before in my little rental cabin, I carefully strung my rod and rigged my leader. I unfurled it to where the sighter met the tippet ring, then considered the calculus of heavy water, the potential for large, and the need to get down deep. Using 4x tippet would certainly be justified in this situation, but it may not sink fast enough. How about 5x? But the thing with 5x is that it's only one one-hundredths of an inch thicker than 6x. Then I reminded myself that 6x was the same setup that slaughtered in the Catskills. Decision made.

I heard the river long before I saw it, a tinny hiss that grew more voluminous with each step. Then I spotted it through gaps in the hardwoods—streaks of whitewater hurrying through the forest. The trail forked above a large pool that looked too deep for the tandem rig, so I decided to continue downriver. Eventually I came to a bend where the rapids slowed and deepened into a craggy run.

I waded to a shallow gravel bar, stripped off line, and popped it through the guides. When the leader and nymphs straightened in the current below me, I pitched them to the head of the run. They sank easily in the softer water, and I led them with the rod.

Twitch. Fish on. I lifted and a seven-inch brook trout bounced on the surface. It felt familiar—the kind of wild brookie I hook in Catskill tributaries. I slid it across the current into my waiting hand, twisted the Frenchy free, and watched it dart away. Cute little thing.

Just as I was about to make another cast, the Voice-of-Responsibility in my head made one last attempt at an intervention. *Maybe you should switch to 4x*, it said. . . . *You hook a large fish in this big water you'll be glad you switched.* . . . *Retying might take three minutes, tops* . . .

I briefly pondered these excellent points while the river seemed to roar even louder around me.

Nah.

I flipped the nymphs back into the run. Then I felt another twitch, raised the rod, and—*oh shit*. A massive brook trout churned and wallowed and gnashed like an enraged crocodile. The three-weight bounced and heaved in my hand. The trout's thick caudal fin found purchase in the current, and the immense fish began to power to the far side of the run. Then—"pop"—the sudden, sickening feeling of parting 6x tippet.

The largest wild brook trout I ever hooked. Was. Gone.

I won't deny that I may have let out an audible shriek or worse. When I checked the leader, the 6x had severed at the dropper knot. Both flies gone. So not only did I just bust off a huge wild brook trout leaving a fly in its mouth, it was now swimming around with some tippet connected to the other Frenchy.

I know. Unforgivable. Indefensible. Inexcusable. Deplorable, even. But I ask you, my fellow anglers, how many of you would have done the exact same thing? Let those without sin cast the first fly. Anyone? Yeah, that's what I thought.

The Bomber and the Brook Trout

A GIANT, MUTILATED TIRE LAID TOPPLED AGAINST A ROCK, THE rusting strut still attached. Fifty feet away, the broken tail-gun section—a pitted aluminum frame with rows of blown-out windows—slumped next to a tree.

More than sixty years earlier, on January 24, 1963, while on a low-altitude training mission, a massive B-52 Stratofortress bomber slammed into Elephant Mountain in the North Woods of Maine. Seven of the nine-member crew died. The two survivors—the pilot and navigator—had to endure minus-thirty-degree temperatures and five feet of snow before they were rescued the following day.

I stood in this somber and eerie place, now a sort of shrine, one August afternoon a few years ago. To find it, I followed a maze of washboard logging roads through various tree plantations and clear-cuts in Maine's ubiquitous commercial timberlands. Eventually, I came to a turnoff across from a metal sign stating plainly: "B52 Memorial." After a short hike up a well-used trail, I found myself among the wreckage. A forest had since grown up around it. Maples and birches, some now a foot or more in diameter and forty feet tall, shouldered aside pieces of fuselage. Drifts of leaf litter and loam blanketed shards of wing.

Somewhere nearby, the ominous collective roar of dozens of chainsaws pierced the woods, a stark reminder that, shrine or no shrine, this was logging land; trees must be cut and sawmills fed. Thoughts swirled in my head: the dead airmen, the forest slowly reclaiming the wrecked bomber; yet more woods about to be laid bare. All the while, the chainsaws grew louder. I made my way back down the trail.

Earlier, on the winding ride up Elephant Mountain, a blue line had appeared on my GPS. I had already been fooled twice by what turned out to be little more than wet spots oozing through foot-wide culverts. But this time, the road briefly dipped and steepened. Hope arose. At the bottom of a hill, a bridge made from eight-by-eight railroad ties clunked loudly under my tires. Below, a twenty-foot-wide stream hurried through thick woods then disappeared around a bend like an apparition. I made a mental note and continued to the crash site.

When I returned, I pulled to the side of the road and shut off the engine. The shrill of chainsaws was gone, replaced by the rush of trout-water. A hermit thrush sang its fluty, haunting song somewhere in the woods behind me.

I grabbed my four-weight already strung with a hair-wing spider, scrambled through shinhopple and shrub dogwood, and wet-waded into the stream. Cool water washed around my knees. My world quickly rendered into green mossy rocks, white foam, and a black-tannin pool.

The first fish attacked more than it rose. So did the next one and the one after that. Six- and seven-inch brook trout, as innocent as newborns, repeatedly launched themselves out of the water attempting to bring down the spider. Some succeeded. They quickly came to hand, black-backed and dark-eyed, with fine red and yellow spots alternating along their sides.

I waded to the next pool. The stream narrowed between two boulders and deepened. I kept low but held the rod high allowing the spider to skate and bounce in the flow. Brookies cartwheeled. They slashed. They swatted. I felt like Thoreau on his first expedition into the Maine woods. Never did a stream feel so untouched.

I released another trout and made another cast. Death, plane crashes, and melancholy had long flowed downstream and away. Sometimes, thankfully, there is another side of the mountain.

ROCKING THE EASTERN STONEFLY HATCH

THEY APPEAR MAGICALLY, LIKE PRESENTS UNDER A CHRISTMAS tree when you were seven years old. One morning in late May, you wade into the stream and behold! Dozens of stonefly husks cling to every rock and boulder. Suddenly, each run, tailout, and slot beckons like an all-you-can-eat buffet. And you are freaking hungry.

Here in the northeast, stoneflies are not nearly as celebrated as the famous salmonfly hatch on western rivers. Yet fast fishing awaits those anglers ready to adapt. Forget graceful, seventy-foot casts with lovely drag-free floats, and trout rising as a Bach sonata plays in the background. Time to knot on some eight-pound Maxima and splatter down big, hairy bugs with graceless hauls. This is fly fishing to Motörhead.

Stoneflies do not prompt Latinizing the way mayflies do. I lump all my springtime stones together as either golden, black, or brown and leave it at that. Someone who sidles up to you at a bar and mentions he is eagerly awaiting the emergence of *Acroneuria lycorias* should probably be avoided. On the other hand, if the guy on the next stool over tells you he just saw a crapload of goldens, immediately ply him with alcohol and lots of it.

Except for the tiny early black stoneflies you sometimes see motor-boating across creeks during winter thaws, most fishable eastern stonefly hatches are later spring occurrences. On my home waters in the Catskills in upstate New York, which includes world-class rivers like the upper Delaware, Beaverkill, and Neversink, I don't expect to see them in any numbers until just before Memorial Day, with mid-June being about peak. And bulk numbers are what you are looking for. There's something about when these bugs seasonally erupt that causes trout to suddenly lock in like crocodiles on the wildebeest migration. Everything from six-inch brookies on tiny mountain tributaries to twenty-inch browns in the big Delaware have at it.

But don't look for traditional blanket hatches either. Though you may see staggering numbers of nymphal husks and newly hatched adults crawling along the shore, eastern stoneflies rarely hit the water all at once. It's mostly one here, one there. Come evening, you may see scatterings of egg-layers crash-landing in riffles, but that's about as abundant as they get. The one exception is on a dry, windy day right after a mass emergence. Then, recently hatched adults can be blown off streamside vegetation by the hundreds before their wings fully dry, and the river will boil with rising fish. But the combination of those perfect conditions happens about once every other leap year. If you stumble onto it, though, feel free to call or text me. Please.

For flies, traditional Stimulators, Sofa Pillows, and their ilk in sizes ten to as large as six certainly work, but my favorite is something I call the Hot Mess. I tie it on a size eight 2XL dry fly hook with a fuzzy body of either olive, cream, or yellow rabbit dubbing. Then I lock in a gob of stacked deer hair and pull it back to form a bullet head. But the last step is crucial: I literally crumple the fly in my hand like a scrap of paper you're about to toss in the garbage. This splays, folds, and kinks the hair-wing making it look like something that splattered on your windshield. Tied correctly, a

Hot Mess doesn't land in the water as much as it flops. And when it does, you twitch, water throws, and a trout leaps.

Speaking of twitches, my own rule is to cast once or maybe twice and let the fly dead drift. If nothing takes, I cast again but check the rod high. When the fly lands (flops), I give it action so it jumps and daps in the current just like a floundering stonefly. I can't tell you how many times that final quiver provokes a vicious take. If I can position myself to skip the bug upstream instead of down, so much the better. For some reason, trout prefer their stones moving against the current, not with it.

Don't wait for risers to show, either. Fish the water. I like rocky riffles, or swift, narrow slots against boulders. On smaller streams, tailouts between plunge pools—particularly if they gather a few bubble lines—are big medicine.

And dammit man, cast. A lot. Put the fly here. Then over there. Twitch it in front of that boulder. Then next to that one. Use drag to your advantage. Think like a stonefly. Make that Hot Mess dance. You are looking for a trout that seems to be waiting its whole life to crush that fly. And when it does, set the hook and I dare you not to air guitar to "The Ace of Spades" with your five-weight.

Halftime at the Cabin

We've owned the cabin for a little more than twenty years now, since 2003. It's perched above a rushing tributary of the East Branch of the Delaware River in the Catskill Mountains. My son grew up splashing in the stream and catching frogs, paddling the river, and hiking in the woods. He starts college in September. Over the years, friends and neighbors have come and gone. Some moved away; others passed. Scattered second homes have sprung up along the dirt road where forests once stood. The fishing, too, has waxed and waned. Droughts and low water seem more and more frequent. Anglers complain that the river is too crowded, and certain hatches are not what they once were. Maybe so. Then, hidden in a hard drive, I find a journal entry.

June 9, 2017—Arrived at the cabin Friday evening. Unpacked, grabbed gear, and drove down to the East Branch. Glimpsed the river from the road and spotted two drift boats bearing down on the eddy I hoped to fish. But they still had a half mile to go, so I sped past them and parked in my usual spot along the road. I barely had enough time to yank on waders, scramble down the bank, and stake out the bubble line I wanted to fish. By then, it was after 8:00 p.m., and a few fish rose here and there. Decent numbers of some sort of chubby charcoal caddis flew about along with a few sulfurs. With the drift boats now closing in, I made a few casts, then hooked and eventually landed a fourteen-inch brown on a ratty-looking Comparadun already rigged to my leader.

Not sure if it was because they saw me release the fish, but one of the boats dropped anchor maybe a hundred feet upstream of me just close enough that I felt slightly cramped. Then all four of us—the guide, his two sports, and I—waited for something to happen. It turned out to be a long wait, with the rises dwindling despite the lowering light. A few spawning shad broke up the monotony, racing around and swirling in the shallows. After maybe twenty minutes, the drift boat captain pulled anchor and rowed on to join his fellow guide who had floated around the next bend.

Just before dark, trout started coming up more frequently. I approached a fish rising on the far side of the bubble line, made a cast, but couldn't make out where the fly landed. The take must have been subtle, because next thing I knew, the line jerked and a nice trout cleared the water, surged, and the hook pulled. Damn.

That turned out to be my last fish of the night. I heard a few sippers in slower water but could now barely see anything and couldn't tell if my casts were inches or feet off the mark. I got off the river at 10:00 and did my own sipping of a smoky whisky by 10:15.

The next morning, I decided to make a pass through the six-foot-wide stream in front of the cabin and was surprised to find a better class of trout than I normally would expect this time of year. I hooked a few genuine eight-to-nine-inch rainbows and landed what may be my best 'bow ever in the stream—a small-headed female pushing ten inches. My hunch is that the higher water this season has kept larger fish in the stream longer. On a typical year, rainbows of that size-class have already migrated to the East Branch. No brookies this time, though I lost what looked like a nicer one alongside a logjam. Saw a few fry, too, so it looks like the last spawn was successful.

Later, after dinner, I headed back to the East Branch around 7:30. It still felt early, so I sat on a rock and waited. No drift boats to contend with this time, thankfully. Shad began to stir again, and a bald eagle swooped so low I could hear the air rushing over its wings. I thought it was going to try to pick off a shad, but it banked at the last minute and flew off. By 8:30 bugs started to get active: the same chubby caddis joined by some sulfurs and the last of the green drakes. Then trout began rising. I made a cast in tricky currents, and the Comparadun started dragging unnaturally. But it must have looked just like a skittering caddis, because a fifteen-inch brown latched on. After I landed it, I saw another fish just downstream now coming up steadily. So I fed the fly down-current and watched it disappear in a small dimple. I set the hook and something powerful tore off a few yards of line, shook its head, then ran some more. A couple of minutes later, I cradled a thick rainbow of seventeen inches or so. By the time I released it, however, most of the other risers had gone quiet. I made a few casts to random sippers, but none took.

It was now 9:20 and the river seemed dead, so I decided to call it an early night. I hiked up the bank and began walking to the car. There was still some silvery light on the water, and I glanced at it while making my way down the road. Then, thirty feet below me, I saw them: two bank sippers gulping down bugs every few seconds. I could tell by the rises—deliberate and authoritative—that these fish were not small.

I stood and watched for a minute. There is no trail to get to the water at this particular spot, and the bank is *steep* and tangled with brush. Plus, it was almost dark. Both fish continued rising. *There will be a time when I physically cannot do this, but it is not yet that time,* I thought to myself. So, I clicked on my headlamp and clambered down the bank trying to avoid dislodging loose boulders and otherwise injuring myself. I succeeded and found myself maybe ten feet from the first fish, which was still gulping away. But it was so close—literally just off my rod tip—that it was hard to correctly present the Comparadun, which by now I could no longer see. So I decided to switch to an enormous Coffin Fly hoping I might at least watch where it landed and track its drift.

I managed to high-stick a tight cast and squinted trying to follow the fly as it dropped to the water. But it vanished in the blackness. I thought to myself: *There was a time when I could have seen that fly land on the river, but that time has passed . . .*

I felt the take before I even saw the rise. The rod jerked, and the fish bolted to the middle of the river sending slack fly line whirling around like a giant piece of spaghetti. A truck may have been easier to stop. Five chaotic seconds later, just as I was about to get the fish on the reel, the Coffin Fly pulled. Damn. Big fish.

All the while, the other fish kept rising. It came up every few seconds in front of a submerged outcropping of bedrock maybe thirty feet downstream. I approached, made an easy cast, and could tell the fly was in its feeding lane. Then I felt a sharp yank and saw a huge splash followed by nothingness. The fish must have sipped in the drake then shook off before I could react.

I stood there for another minute looking for more rises, but it was over, at least from where I stood. By now it was ten o'clock and the sky was filled with stars. I scaled the bank like some wader-clad mountaineer. Then I tossed my rod in the grass along the road, grabbed onto weeds and saplings, and pulled myself onto level ground. I brushed myself off and glanced back at the spot, happy I can still fish such godforsaken places.

When I got back to the cabin, I poured a whisky and watched a Luna moth pirouetting around the porch light.

Here's to twenty more years.

PART II

In Home Waters

I don't want you pacing around here all day. Get out and fish somewhere.

—My wife, last week

Bluelining Dirty Jersey

Let's be clear: no one is going to cancel their annual trip to the Bighorn or the Madison to spend a week on Hakihokake Creek. Or Beatty's Brook for that matter. Or any of the few dozen wild trout streams you've never heard of that run through my home state of New Jersey.

Yeah, that's right, New Jersey. Dirty Jersey. Home of *The Sopranos* and Bon Jovi. Yet here in our most densely populated state, an oddball gallery of lightly fished, wild trout waters persist and even thrive. Some are tiny rills that twist through remnant alder swamps. Others tumble past woodlands and fallow farm fields. Still others hide in plain sight—hard by roaring interstates or behind condo complexes. Trout rise, eighteen-wheelers jake brake, leaf blowers wail, all oblivious to each other.

I'll admit, these streams are not for everyone. The trout are often small and skittish, the casts sometimes impossible, the access tricky. It's no wonder most local fly anglers looking for wild fish pack their gear, point their cars north to the Catskills or west to Pennsylvania, and zoom past these creeks unaware of their very existence. Yet in their own way, they are every bit as challenging as the so-called destination rivers.

I began bluelining in New Jersey during COVID and continue to learn new streams. I use the standard methods: publicly available stream-survey data and satellite maps. Add a travel mug of decent coffee and a half tank of gas and I'm on my way.

Then I explore. In this sanitized, digital age, the often messy, inefficient act of roaming around with no idea what you might find, the back of the car rattling with rod tubes and assorted gear, is pure fun.

I have hit dead ends, I'll freely admit. Sometimes it's a one-hundred-yard-wide thicket of wader-shredding multiflora rose standing between me and the stream with no obvious trail or other access point. Other times a gauntlet of posted signs glares back at me, and I can almost feel the wilting look of an already pissed-off landowner staring from somewhere afar. I drive on.

And then sometimes the trout simply forget to show. Some expeditions to prime-looking streams with supposed high trout populations draw hard skunkings. It happens. So I drive on some more.

But then I strike gold: a stream tumbling from a cleft in a hillside, complete with an easy-on-easy-off parking area. It turns out to be filled with wild brook trout tucked in the shadows of boulders deposited from the last ice age. They take a parachute anything and are bedazzled with the usual riot of haloed red spots, ivory-tipped pectorals, olive worm-track back—the works.

I briefly hold a seven-inch brookie in my hand. Icy water purls around the fish and my fingers. How many millennia have its ancestors eked out a living on this little stream? What have they witnessed? First the mighty Wisconsin glacier that receded four-teen thousand years ago leaving behind this clear, flowing water. Then, who knows? Wooly mammoths? Giant sloths? The Lenni Lenape Indians? Retreating Redcoats? It's humbling to release a trout whose ancestors have been here for untold centuries longer than my own.

Then there is the brown trout stream that, from the road, looks butt-ugly, complete with a composting couch dumped along its banks. But walk upstream for a half mile and you emerge into a magical bottomland of towering sycamores and tulip poplars with the creek winding through the middle of it. Wild browns rise here tight to root-wads and overhanging cover. They require triple-black diamond casts. Sometimes I just sit on the bank and watch the trout come up, contemplating the impossible geometry it would take to shoot a fly into a feeding lane. If I'm smart, I'll remain seated and enjoy the simple spectacle of a wild trout in its element and leave it at that. But inevitably, I succumb to temptation and execute a cast above my skill set that promptly winds up stuck in a malicious branch or evil tree root. The trout is gone. Thanks for playing.

There's a meadow stream I know walled in by willows that runs behind a strip mall. It is no more than ten feet wide. I came to a pool where a nice trout rose steadily at the tailout to skittering caddis. It was early afternoon, and I was determined to catch this fish. So I crouched low, took a deep breath, and had at it. Ninety minutes later, I sat sprawled on a rock with a half dozen flies broken off somewhere in the willow branches around me. My leader, frayed and tattered, swung aimlessly in the current. The trout continued happily rising. I had missed it twice, and it was now ignoring everything I cast. I couldn't take it anymore, so I stood up and spooked it out of spite. Only on the mighty Upper Delaware with its PhD trout had I spent more time on a single fish. As a footnote, I returned a week later and hooked the same trout on maybe the third cast. It promptly powered into a snag, hung up the fly, and shook free. It might have been twelve inches long. I stood there head down, crushed, never once thinking: who cares, it's only a little trout from New Jersey.

By the way, foot-long wild trout are the exception here, not the rule. Most are half that size, maybe slightly larger. And while I have been surprised by a few relative bruisers up to fifteen or even sixteen inches, that's not really what I am after. The commodity here is not "sticking pigs," it's solitude. And that's what these streams consistently deliver. I guess few anglers are willing to put up with crawling around on your hands and knees, endless snags, and Joe Humpreys's sniper casts—all for a seven-inch brown. And I am so okay with that.

In fact the only real competition I've seen on these wild streams comes from occasional great blue herons, kingfishers, and mergansers. I've seen tracks that look like mink, so maybe those, too. The rare time I see another car in a turnout, I drive on. I do this both as a courtesy to the angler who got there first, and because I've read that great blue herons don't share fishing spots. So I won't either if I can help it. And besides often there is another creek the next valley over with no one there.

Just recently, I worked the problem and got off a magical, trigonometric cast to a steady riser coming up in a tight pool. The stream itself is best described as moderately funky, meandering behind a large housing development before disappearing under a noisy highway. The CDC caddis touched down just on the far side of a submerged, fallen tree worn smooth. On a previous trip, I swung and missed at this fish putting it down for the rest of the session. This time the trout tilted up and ate with heartbreaking confidence. I came tight and hard, forcing it to clear the tree and head into open water. And then it was mine.

In my hand lay a fourteen-inch wild brown trout, an improbable fish born and bred in this improbable stream. How audacious that it lives here. How *dare* it. New Jersey has thrown everything at this fish: over-development, invasive species, climate change, and still it survives. And now it was glaring at me with its knowing eyes, the caddis hanging from its jaw, as if saying, *That's all you got?*

I backed the fly out and released my grip. The trout immediately darted beneath the submerged tree, its home. I considered the pool for a while and what just happened and decided I won't cast here for the rest of the season; there would be no point. Just knowing that this ballsy, wild trout lives here, now thumbing its pectorals at me, was more than enough.

WHY I DIG STOCKERS

THE HONEY-COLORED BAMBOO FOUR-WEIGHT SWISHES THROUGH sweet spring air. The line straightens, and a brace of wet flies touches down in the slick behind a submerged boulder. The rod is raised slightly, sending the flies slowly swimming across the current. A second later, the leader twitches, and a trout is hooked. An eleven-inch rainbow jumps, then bores for the bottom before surrendering to an outstretched hand.

But now, instead of a gentle release, the trout is grabbed with the authority of an osprey. With the rod tucked under one arm, a hanging chain stringer is pulled from a wading belt. The rattle of aluminum pierces the air as the trout thrashes. But not for long. With a quick grab and pull, the fish is gilled, and a cloud of blood billows in the current and washes downstream. The rainbow now hangs in the stream lifeless, along with three other trout already dead and bled out.

A scene from a modern trout angler's nightmare? No, it's how I spent last Saturday.

You see, the trout was stocked, and I am an unabashed lover of hatchery trout. Yes, stockers, rubber trout, hatchery product, or whatever you wish to call them. The ones with the washed-out colors and crinkled pectorals raised in concrete raceways and fed pellets; the ones that are tossed literally by the millions into countless rivers, creeks, and ponds across the United States. Yep, those ones, and I love to catch them—and I love to take them home.

But before you string me up with fly-line or tar and feather me with saddle hackles, please know that I, presumably like you, am hopelessly in love with wild trout and the magical places where they live. My stream cred includes barbless flies, rubber release nets, and a portfolio of hero shots of me lovingly releasing pea-gravel-born, full-finned fishes. Yet my love of stockers rages on. And here are the reasons why.

1. More casting, less driving. Yes, wild trout are things of untold beauty. But unless you happen to live in the Alaskan bush or Montana's Madison Valley, prepare to rack up some miles chasing them. That's because high-quality wild trout fisheries are usually found in unpeopled areas: remote headwater streams, or "destination rivers"—the kind with five-hour drives, motel stays, or sleeping in the back of the truck. Hatchery fish, on the other hand, are stocked largely out of convenience—the more popular and more accessible the waterway, the more it gets stocked. In my home state of New Jersey, which liberates some six hundred thousand trout each year, some rivers receive literally tens of thousands of trout every spring. Many flow through suburbs, local parks, and other easily accessed areas. One stream I used to live near was within walking distance. To grab a rod after work for a few casts before dinner was both liberating and good for the soul.

2. Good eats. There used to be a Doritos commercial with the tagline: "Crunch all you want; we'll make more." It's kind of like that with hatchery trout—they are stocked expressly for you, the angler, to take home and eat. So please partake. For those who might turn up their noses at the thought of pellet-fed hatchery trout, two words: smoke 'em. Stocked trout—particularly when they are brined with kosher salt and brown sugar then smoked with applewood—are a downright delicious, guilt-free pleasure.

Friends, family, and neighbors love them, too, and never once did I hear anyone say, "Ewwwww, this tastes like a *hatchery* trout."

3. Embrace your inner hunter-gatherer. Catch-and-release fishing may be the single-most important management tool ever invented for recreational fishing. But guess what: it's okay to take some fish home now and then. And it is part of the tradition of angling. Believe it or not, wicker creels—those things Martha Stewart likes to stuff with dried flowers and hang on walls, were originally used to hold fish and keep them cool. Gutting and gilling a fish streamside is fun—in a caveman sort of way—and walking back to your truck with a full creel or stringer feels deeply satisfying. Honoring a trout by killing it quickly and humanely, then taking care of the catch so it doesn't spoil, and finally cooking it and sharing it with friends and family, is beautiful and poetic.

4. Pretend trout streams. Wouldn't it be great if all those pretty-looking streams that run cold and bank-full in the early spring actually held trout year-round? Well, sadly most of them don't. But for a few glorious months, they are de facto trout streams, with plenty of (stocked) fish, and sometimes even decent insect hatches. Who cares if come July they become the domain of smallmouth and sunnies? Try fishing them when they are cold and lovely. A few years back I hit a massive Hendrickson hatch on a popular stocked river that ran through a picturesque village. I parked behind a hardware store and shuffled down to the stream and had classic dry fly fishing for ninety minutes until the hatch petered out. Not once, as trout rose all around me and Hendricksons danced in the air did I ever think, "Well, hell, this isn't real."

5. Break out the fancy flies. You know those flies you may have received from well-meaning family members as gifts—the ones that actually come in little blister packs labeled "Ten Quality Trout Flies"? Or how about those rejects from the tying vise—experiments that went horribly wrong, or flies tied in strange colors from the fly shop bargain bin? Guess what? Hatchery trout love them (so do wild trout under certain conditions, but let's not go there). So fill your fly box and load up.

6. Become a heretic. This may be sacrilege, but how about forgetting the fly rod altogether and go back to the roots, which for many of us means spinning gear or—gasp—bait. Tossing a shiny Mepps on an ultralight or feeling the rat-tat-tat as a fresh stocker gobbles up a worm might just bring you back to carefree days when trout fishing was less about $800 rods and more about simple fun. And who cares if the fish takes the bait deep, or has a face-full of treble hooks—it's coming home with you, remember? (See reason 2.)

7. The four-pound brookie. I unfortunately have no immediate plans to go to Labrador so therefore will not be catching a four-pound wild brook trout anytime soon. But hatchery fish, that's another story. A few years ago, a friend who was a gifted fly caster and fly tier joined me on a stocked stream and caught a twenty-two-inch beast on a spinner. Though hatchery trout can often look washed out, this one was a true looker with an olive worm-track back, full kype, and broad ivory-tipped pectoral fins. My friend has since passed away, and I cherish the photo I have of him smiling and holding his Labrador-sized brookie.

8. Opening Day. It's become hip among serious fly anglers to scorn opening day of trout season as "amateur day," when the great unwashed hordes descend onto stocked streams with Walmart rods and PowerBait. All true. But instead of shuttering yourself indoors and spitefully reading Ernest Schwiebert books, celebrate the opener. It's spring for God's sake, and the rivers are full and trout-some. Grab the kids, head out early, and grab a spot. You'll see everything from guys with surf tackle to four-year-olds with Sponge Bob push-button rods. Lines will wind up in trees, dogs will bark, and people will fall in. Some fish will be caught. It's one big goofy fish-themed party—be part of it.

9. Vigilante fishing. If you are a wild trout purist, then you probably hate it when the stocking truck pulls up to your favorite stream and dumps in a mess of rubber trout. And for good reason: stockers are genetically inferior, can introduce disease, and often outcompete their wild brethren. Here's where you come in: get the hatchery fish the hell out of there. Though it might be more efficient to petition your local fish and game folks not to stock a wild trout stream in the first place, why not have some fun in the meantime, not to mention a few meals?

10. The gateway fish. The first trout I ever caught on a rod and reel was stocked in a stream that runs bathtub warm by the summer. I caught it on a worm, and I rode my bike there with two of my friends. That fish—a ten-inch fresh-from-the-hatchery brown—marked the beginning of a journey that has taken me from Alaska to Tierra del Fuego in pursuit of big wild trout and salmon. I fish for them with flies I lovingly tie myself on elegant fly rods and precision reels. I shudder to think where I would have wound up if, instead of that stocker, I had caught a carp or a chub, or maybe nothing at all. Maybe I'd be golfing.

This spring, literally millions of hatchery trout will once again be released into local waterways. For the savvy angler who can set aside their bias against the lowly stocker, bounty and fun await you. So have at it. Just don't forget the chain stringer.

A Winter Afternoon

It snowed again last Thursday adding another five or six inches to the twenty already on the ground. By Sunday, the late February sun dusted itself off and icicles began to drip, drip, drip. The thermometer outside read thirty-five degrees. I convinced myself this was in fact almost forty, so I grabbed my gear and headed out.

I chose a small, overlooked wild trout stream that straddles the frontier between hard-core New Jersey suburbia and its remnant woodlands. I parked at a dead-end road adjacent to a small county park, tugged on waders, and traversed an enormous pile of snow left behind by the town plow.

Someone snowshoed here recently, so I followed their tracks through the woods—it beat trudging through untrammeled knee-deep snow. After a while, they merged with a cross-country skier's trail, which eventually deposited me at a sharp bend in the stream. A ten-foot-wide ribbon of dark water babbled through an otherwise silent snowscape. The creek ran low and clear; most of its flow remained frozen and locked up in the drifts around me.

For the first quarter mile, I had one sharp pluck on a weighted bugger drifted through a pocket but nothing else. But then I came to a slower, deeper pool with a lazy bubble line moseying into a tailout. I stopped and watched. A few early brown stoneflies and midges wandered on the snow along the banks. I looked closer and could see dark specks drifting in the film. And then, by God, a trout rose. I immediately hunched into stealth mode. The trout rose again pushing a little water. Decent fish. What had begun as a casual afternoon slinging junk had suddenly gotten serious.

I clipped off the streamer and retied with a size 20 Adams. Staying low, I approached the pool and carefully pulled off some fly line. Then, just as I was about to make a cast, I heard from behind me an enthusiastic "Hi!"

I turned around and saw two women with trekking poles standing on the bank maybe thirty feet away.

"Catch anything?" one of them asked.

"No not yet," I said. Then they started to head upstream directly toward the riser, which had just come up again.

I quickly added, "But there's a trout feeding in that pool."

I pointed just as the fish rose. "Do you see it?" I asked.

They stopped and looked. It came up again. "See it right there?"

But they didn't, and I realized some will go through their entire lives and never see a trout sipping midges. Then I asked if they would mind if I made a few casts before they walked past. "Sure!" they said, probably assuming I would immediately catch this mystery fish they couldn't see.

But this was no dumb stocker waiting to be spoon-fed a Power Nugget. It was a wild brown rising cautiously in a tough spot just a few feet from a tailout. One bad cast and faster water would swallow line and leader and send one's fly whirligiging through the pool. Alas, this turned out to be a self-fulfilling prophecy. On my first cast, the fly rooster-tailed directly over the fish. For good measure and perhaps feeling the pressure of an audience, I somehow made the exact same cast again and the trout quit rising.

I turned, thanked them both for their patience, and wished them a pleasant trek. They waved and said something that I couldn't hear over the rush of the stream. Maybe it was how I might consider throwing more slack with an upstream curve cast next time. Not sure. I backed out of the casting position and considered my options. Though the sun was starting to slide lower on the horizon, there was still plenty of fishing time left. And it was pleasant along the stream in those wintry woods. So I leaned up against a fallen tree along the bank and waited. A few bugs still trickled in the current, so maybe the trout would come up again.

Ten minutes later it did. My shoulders tensed, and I eased back to my casting position. I stripped off a couple of arm lengths of line and considered once again the geometry to make the proper presentation. If I piled up the tippet and immediately mended, I could probably. . . . Then I heard a low "thump, thump, thump" growing steadily louder. I turned around just in time to see another trekker coming up the bank. He was moving fast, decked out in a technical ski jacket, breathable pants that audibly swished, and knee-high boots.

"How's it going?" he asked in a blur of flying snow. Before I could answer, he galumphed past, putting down the rising trout before continuing around the next bend. He was gone before I could answer weakly: "Great."

I backed out to my now familiar log and waited some more. Now with some time to kill, I decided to paw through my midge box to see if there was something that might be a better match than the Adams. And there it was. Hidden among tricos and size 22 olives was a speck of a dark caddis—perhaps a 28, the smallest fly in my box and the best match for the electron-sized midges and pencil-tip stones I could still see crawling and flying about. With supreme confidence, I reached for what was clearly *the* fly. But somehow, I fumbled and the tiny caddis dropped into the stream. For a nano-second, it swirled in an eddy behind my wading boot before the current grabbed it and sucked it into the purgatory where all lost flies must go.

I grabbed a size 20 Griffith's Gnat, tied it on, and waited some more. A few minutes later, the trout came up again. By now, I knew the routine: crouch, approach, kneel, cast. I stripped off line, false cast once, then dropped the fly. Somehow, I misfired yet again, overshooting a good three feet past the rising trout to the far bank. I suck. On the next cast, I overcompensated placing the fly impotently into dead-water just a rod's length away. I continued to suck. I picked up the fly one more time and put it maybe a foot below the trout. Still off the mark but better. I decided to let it sit before I picked it up for another cast. It drifted a few inches then began to slowly V-wake. The trout turned and took it down. I lifted the rod and was in.

Like I said, it was a decent fish, and it surged a few times before eventually surrendering. Let's say it was better than ten inches. In fact, all things considered, let's make it eleven. Tomorrow it might be a foot. In any case, it eventually rolled on its side showing off handsome red spots with the little waterlogged Griffith's Gnat hanging from its lower jaw.

I released it and leaned back against the fallen tree for a few moments, breathing in clean winter air. Then I climbed up the snowy bank until I found the cross-country trail, then the snowshoe tracks that eventually led to my car.

THE GIVING STUMP

SOMETIMES, CATCH-AND-RELEASE FLY FISHING CAN FEEL ALMOST dogmatic, with unending imagery of anglers coddling gamefish just before a preordained release, so it can "fight another day." But I do get it: putting fish back may be the single-most effective act of individual conservation we can take. So, it admittedly feels kind of weird when I occasionally land a legal fish, then kill it and take it home for dinner.

Usually, it's an American shad from the Delaware River, caught in early April and full of migratory fat, and vastly underrated as a seasonal food. I sauté the roe and broil the fillets, though sometimes I pickle them, which dissolves its many bones. Or it could be a big, oily surf-caught bluefish, scoffed by many as "too fishy," but wonderful if bled and iced then converted into sashimi or ceviche. I may even take home a limit of stocked rainbows for my smoker. My own dogma is that no wild trout will ever be clamped to my chain stringer, and I refuse to kill a "keeper" striped bass until their population has recovered (it's heading in the other direction, sadly). Ethics, unlike regulations, can be subjective, and yours may vary from mine.

Whatever the catch, my ritual is to clean the fish on a makeshift fillet table on my back deck. When I'm done, I walk to the edge of my yard with the carcass and carefully place it on the stump of an old pin oak. By the next morning, and without fail, the remains are gone without so much as a scale or drop of blood. Which type of critter vacuums up the offering, I am not positive. I suspect a fox, since I sometimes hear its horrific "vixen scream" late at night. But I suppose the visitor could also be a racoon, skunk, or opossum. Currently no black bears live in my area, though that could change. Hopefully it's not a swarm of rats.

I began doing this more than a decade ago when I first moved into this suburban New Jersey home with a half-acre of woods behind it. Rather than freeze the carcass and later dump it in the garbage where it would putrefy in a landfill, I wanted to recycle it back into the natural world. So I presented it to nature, and nature gladly accepted.

Sometimes I think about that first wildlife encounter, with the stump piled high with fish parts. I like to picture a fox, maybe down on its luck from a poor day of hunting squirrels, stumbling upon this dripping heap of riches. Synapses fire in its brain. Maybe it squeals a little. Then, it takes multiple trips to drag the carcass and pieces of fins and offal back to its den. Perhaps it then teaches its kits that no matter what, they must always investigate this amazing stump because, sometimes, the heavens shine down with great gifts.

My own version of the giving stump is a certain logjam on the lower reaches of a nearby unstocked trout stream. The water here is marginal, with much of it running next to a busy interstate. But it is also convenient and thus I fish there often. I've come to learn that a ten-inch brown is a good fish for the stream, and twelve inches is a beast. But then, on a raw November day three years ago, my friend Dee knelt before a tangled mass of fallen tree limbs and dropped a weighted bugger an inch off the wood. She twitched it once then set on a fish that made us both gasp. The fight was brief but intense with several surges that strained the 4x tippet. Eventually it came to her net—a sixteen-inch heavy male.

We clicked away with our phones, marveling at its kype and dark flanks before the release (preordained, of course).

Since then, I have fished the stream dozens of times and always—always—pitch a bugger to the logjam just like Dee did and let it swing in its shadows. Sometimes I am rewarded with an average trout, though usually I catch nothing. I patiently await the next sixteen-incher because I believe in the logjam the same way the fox believes in the stump. Someday the heavens will shine upon both of us once again.

SUCKERS IN A POOL

WHEN I WAS IN TENTH GRADE, I BOUGHT A FIBERGLASS FLY ROD and Pflueger Medalist reel and decided to try my luck fly fishing for trout. It felt like a natural progression, having already spin-fished for bluegills in ponds, and bait-cast for bass and pickerel in lakes. Now it was time to cast flies into rivers for pretty fish that ate bugs. But I knew little about how to catch trout, except from what I had gleaned from a few *Field and Stream* articles with banner headlines like "Ten Tips for Giant 'Bows!"

I pedaled my bike to a local, stocked stream a few miles from my parents' house in suburban New Jersey, then wandered along the banks making tentative casts with a wet fly. Eventually, I came to a slow pool with an old flood control wall slumped against the far shoreline. I picked my way along, gazing into the clear water. To my joy, I spotted a dozen large fish holding in the shadow of the wall. Some looked nearly two feet long. Clearly, it was a school of the enormous rainbows I had been reading about.

I stripped out line and made a down-and-across cast bracing for a hard strike. But the fish ignored the fly. So I cast again. Still nothing. I cast again and again and again. Nothing. Nothing. Nothing. I changed flies, twitching them inches away from the fishes' snouts. Utter indifference. It was as if the fish were zombies or perhaps river rocks shaped like trout. Then an older angler walked up to the pool with a spinning rod.

"Get any?" he asked.

I told him no but excitedly pointed out the school of huge trout.

He looked in the water, sneered, and said, "Those aren't trout! They're suckers!" With a laugh, he added: "They don't hit!"

Cue the sad trombone . . .

At that point in my young angling career, I admit I hadn't even heard of suckers. Now I knew these large zombie-fish were apparently not even worth a cast. Just the name alone sounded like something to avoid—suckers . . . gross!

But it turns out the old man was wrong about them not hitting. Kind of. Suckers do occasionally grab weighted nymphs—usually to the chagrin of a high-sticking trout angler. Friends have told me stories of hooking what at first they thought was the trout of a lifetime, only to see an oversize brownish-yellow fish loll on the surface with their fly dangling from its namesake suction-cup mouth. Or sometimes they would foul-hook one on a streamer stripped near the bottom. After an initial panicked surge, the fish would flag revealing the ruse. More sad trombone. Damn suckers.

One time, I decided to try to eat one. It was mid-March, and I heard that suckers staged at creek mouths prior to spawning, and that early season fish were not bad eating. So, a friend and I packed in a camp stove and skillet to where a large stream entered the Delaware River. Since this was a meat trip, I drifted a worm with a split shot and soon had a solid take. After what I can best describe as a forgettable fight, I landed a sixteen-incher that I bonked on the head and filleted. Then I sautéed it in onions and bacon, and we ate it shore-lunch style. It was firm and flaky, and pretty soon we had devoured everything except its unscaled skin.

Kind of tasty, those suckers.

The fish we ate that day was a white sucker, a ubiquitous species found from Labrador to New Mexico. But there are many other kinds. It turns out North America is the Amazon rainforest for sucker diversity, with some seventy-eight of the world's eighty known species found here. Angling author and fishing friend Matt Miller, a proud sucker champion and advocate, says his favorite is the largescale sucker found in his local waters in Idaho. He describes it as hard fighting and aggressive, yet difficult to fool. His holy grail, though, is the blue sucker, which he hasn't yet caught and describes as perhaps a more difficult fish to hook than Atlantic salmon. Matt also points out that many sucker species require clean, free-flowing rivers, just like native trout, salmon, and steelhead, and are therefore impacted by the usual suspects—dams, dewatering for irrigation, and climate change. Ergo, if you protect suckers and their habitat, you may be safeguarding other more celebrated "gamefish," too.

So, suckers are kind of cool.

Several decades after that first try with a fly rod, I recently found myself prospecting along an unstocked and overlooked wild trout stream. On a previous trip, I had released a few ten-inch browns but felt that the creek, which featured deep logjams and mysterious undercut banks, may have been holding out on me. The water ran low and clear that day, with a bright sun bearing down—bad conditions for fooling wild trout. I eventually came to a slow run, and there on the bottom, perhaps fifty white suckers had gathered. The fish, semi-spooked by my presence, periodically dashed around the pool and reordered their ranks like a version of musical chairs.

Then I saw it. Holding among the suckers swam a large wild brown—easily twenty inches long. The big trout had presumably taken up with the sucker school to protect itself—a safety-in-numbers strategy. Without the suckers as cover, it would have certainly been holed up deep in a logjam or under the bank, where I never would have seen it. I didn't bother casting to the nervous fish, but now I knew its precise address. I would return on a better day, perhaps when the water was high and stained, armed with a weighted streamer. Or I could dead drift an egg fly when the suckers spawn in the riffles and the trout would hold behind them scarfing down dislodged eggs. Or maybe I'd wait for a spinner fall and stalk the big brown sipping spent mayflies at last light. Whichever the case, I filed the location in a lockbox that I would open at a day and time of my choosing.

And for that I say: thank you suckers.

THE NEIGHBORHOOD
BROOKIE

FORTY YEARS AGO, IN THE MID-1980S WHEN I WAS EIGHTEEN OR nineteen, I became obsessed with an enormous stuffed brook trout hanging on the wall inside a house a few blocks from where my parents lived. I spotted it one night while walking home from my summer job at the local supermarket. It was bathed in warm lamp light above what looked like the mantel in a den. From the sidewalk, I could see its arced olive back and open mouth as if perpetually rising to suck down a Royal Wulff or Adams.

From that point on, whenever I walked past, I would try to steal glimpses of the big trout. Sometimes the shades were drawn, and I would grumble as I walked by, disappointed. But when they were open, I would stop and marvel. The trout became a keyhole into an untamed world far from the monoculture of the New Jersey suburbs I called home.

One night after dinner, my high school friend Greg, who lived a few houses away, called and asked if I wanted to go for a walk in the neighborhood. These were regular occurrences; Greg would stop by, and we would head down to the local school. Then he would smoke a joint, and we would wander the streets for hours. I didn't smoke myself, but enjoyed Greg's THC-fueled rants about important things like obscure tracks on the Clash's *Sandinista* triple album, or how much he hated Ronald Reagan.

On this particular night, we found ourselves straying from our usual route. We turned a corner, and I realized we were approaching the house with the enormous trout. I told this to Greg, and though he wasn't an angler, he nevertheless became extremely interested, probably due in no small part to being stoned.

We stopped in front of the house—a stately white center colonial—and I gazed once more at the brookie, which looked as magnificent as ever. Then Greg said, "Let's ring the doorbell and ask them about the fish."

"No way," I said. "They'll think we're creepy stalkers."

"C'mon, let's do it!" he said, as if this was now the most important decision we would ever make for the rest of our lives.

Throughout high school, Greg had a knack for talking me into things I didn't want to do, like randomly calling popular girls from our classes, or stupidly trying cigarettes. So, the next thing I knew, I rang the doorbell, and we stood there on the steps waiting. A few moments later, a well-dressed woman in her fifties answered.

"Can I help you?" she asked.

I swallowed, and stammered: "Um . . . hi . . . I've been noticing that big brook trout on the wall in your house and wanted to ask you about it."

The woman looked at us slightly puzzled.

Then Greg pointed at me and added: "This guy is a fishing *nut*." Nut indeed.

Another pause. Then the woman smiled and said, "Sure. Come on inside."

Stunned and thrilled, the next thing I knew, we were both standing in a cozy, well-appointed den just two feet away from the giant brookie. Up close, it was even more spectacular than I imagined, a perfect old-school skin mount with a matte finish. Each speckle, haloed spot, and vermiculation painted in exquisite detail. The woman said it weighed five pounds, then she proudly told the story of how she caught it in Labrador with her first husband. I nodded as she spoke, enchanted. With every word, I could smell the tang of balsam and see wild northern rivers filled with huge rising fish.

Then I noticed something else hanging on another wall that looked like it came from some sort of billfish, so I asked about that, too.

"Oh, that's a swordfish bill!" she said, delighted that I'd noticed. And then she regaled us with a Hemingway-like tale of battling the big billfish, again caught in the company of her first husband.

Meanwhile, husband number 2 stood ten feet away, arms folded and silent. Clearly, he was not amused by the two teenagers standing in his den and chatting with his wife—Greg with his earring and stringy, long hair, and me with my regulation spikey punk crew cut.

But she ignored him, and we continued to talk. And though I personally could have stayed there all night, eventually it was time to leave. We thanked her over and over for telling us about her trophies, and she in turn thanked us for stopping by so she could relive them once again. Like the giant stuffed brook trout forever arcing upward, all anglers, when asked about a big fish from their past, will apparently rise to anyone, anywhere, anytime.

Tales from the Dark Side

Last week I went to the dark side. Briefly. For precisely one day, I fished with spinning gear on some wild trout streams here in New Jersey. It was legal of course; none of the water was fly fishing only. But still . . .

It all started when I discovered a YouTuber from neighboring Pennsylvania who specializes in throwing spinners on small streams for shockingly large wild browns. I wound up binge-watching video after video that showed him pitch hardware deep into some wood or alongside an undercut bank and hook another twenty-two-incher. I couldn't look away.

And it got me thinking. Perhaps I had been missing out on something in my local streams—particularly the ones with juicy logjams with complex currents where I could only scratch the surface with weighted streamers. Sure, I coaxed an occasional twelve-inch fish from these spots, but maybe somewhere down in that gnarled abyss, far beyond where I could practically reach with my five-weight, a true beast lurked, ready to pounce on something with mighty swinging blades.

Even if I didn't hook anything on hardware, maybe I would move a big fish so I could return later to fish for it properly with my fly rod. Or so I convinced myself. So, I dusted off a light-action smallmouth rod and stopped at a local Dick's where I bought a couple of size 2 gold Mepps—the preferred ammo of the YouTuber.

I knew the first stream well. It wound through bottomlands of sycamore, silver maple, and tulip poplar. A few weeks earlier, I landed a genuine seventeen-incher on a twitched tungsten bugger and spooked an even larger fish. The stream ran stained and a little high—perfect for something big and flashy. I approached a deep, slow-moving pool with a fallen silver maple lodged against the far bank and made an underhand cast. The spinner plunked down, and I let it sink for a second or two. Then I gave the rod a twitch, and the blade began thrumming along. Halfway into the retrieve, I felt a light hit and saw a fifteen-inch brown glide back underneath the trunk looking unimpressed. The fish never returned for a second look, and I began thinking that a wooly bugger, with its pulsating marabou tail, would have been crushed. But all my streamers were back home.

I moved upstream and began to follow boot tracks from another angler who had apparently already hit virtually every pool I wanted to fish. I guessed they had been through the day before, and even though that probably didn't impact the fishing, it still made me feel like I was feeding off crumbs. Perhaps it was another spinner-slinger who already laid the stream bare. Or a thoughtful fly angler who methodically picked the stream apart. In any case, all the other pools I fished were empty despite a thorough carpet-bombing with hardware. So I moved on.

The next stream ran stained but not particularly high—tough conditions for small water and skittish wild trout. And predictably the fishing was slow with several usually productive pools barren. I'm not sure if the trout were turned off by the big spinner flopping into the pool like a dead bat, or they were just turned off in general. But then I wound up landing the first fish of the trip: an eleven-inch wild brown holding in a pool so tight I normally skip it with my fly rod. Turned out it was easier to pitch a spinner beneath drooping branches of poison ivy than it is to roll cast a bugger in there. So, at least there was that.

The last stream of the day flowed through a mixed woodland. Ironically, in the first pool I approached, three steady risers sipped midges along a bubble line. But my midge box was . . . well, you know where it was. I decided not to insult rising wild trout with my caveman gear, so I moved on to the next run. There, things picked up. I took four small trout one after another. It was mechanically easy—just fling out the spinner, crank a few turns, and hook a trout. Between casts, I imagined how fun it would have been to dead-drift a Zebra Midge or soft hackle. The last fish wound up being the best one of the day—a twelve-incher—ten inches short of the YouTuber's average. Unfortunately, the gaff-sized treble, though de-barbed, had lodged deeply. I managed to ease the hooks out, drawing just a little blood, and the trout seemed to swim away strongly. On that note, I left. The spinning rod went back in the garage and the spinners in a tackle box.

I'm sure things would have felt different if I did in fact land a twenty-plus-incher like the YouTuber. But I didn't, so my opinion of spin fishing for wild trout on small streams remains the same: it's kind of like eating a gas station burrito—easy and convenient, but afterward you'll probably regret it.

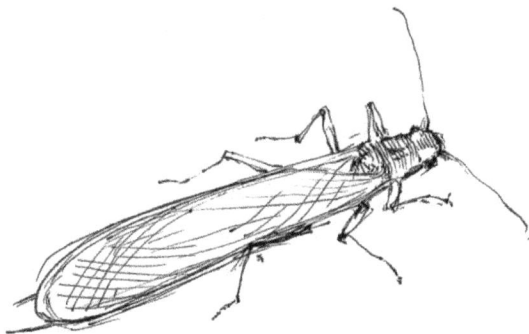

PART III

BETWEEN CASTS

What the hell is a green drake?

—MY BROTHER, 2013

It's Time for a Slow Fish Movement

"Prob hooked fifty."

The words felt strange as I tapped out a quick report on my phone to my friend Dave. But it was true. I had spent the better part of the afternoon Euronymphing, and the fishing was indeed ridiculous. Within the first hour, I had already hooked more than a dozen; by hour two, I lost count. Wild browns—nice fish up to eighteen inches—with a few thick, foot-long brookies thrown in. In the evening, I switched to twitching attractors in some faster runs and landed another ten or so until I finally quit at dark.

By the time I hit send, the day had become just a blur of hooksets, thrashing fish, and rapid-fire releases. A few hasty photos of larger trout cradled in my half-submerged left hand served as documentation of the day, but little else. Any poetry of a perfect cast, soft take, or arcing leap was lost in the sheer numbers of fish.

Before last season began, I found myself with the unshakeable urge to make my fishing days more "epic." Maybe it was certain ads in fishing magazines that said I needed to "Crush Variables," or that "Failure Was Not an Option." Or videos that showed cool-looking dudes repeatedly hooking up and fist-bumping in high-def. Whatever it was, my own modest fishing success suddenly felt anemic. It was time to up my game.

First, I made key purchases: top-of-the line prescription sunglasses with low-light lenses; wading boots with carbide studs that I individually tightened with a socket wrench and drop of super glue; a heavy-duty collapsible wading staff in a sort of quiver that I could unsheathe like a samurai sword. Then I tied dozens and dozens of tungsten-beaded nymphs and CDC everything and inserted them in my fly box like bullets in an ammo clip. I studied and learned new super-fast knots and read about ways to swap out leaders more efficiently as conditions changed. Previously "lucky" fishing shirts were replaced with camouflage hoodies so I could melt into streamside vegetation.

By opening day, I had transformed into an angler-assassin.

And it paid off, I guess. The new gear allowed me to approach fish I had surely been missing or spooking, and the techniques I learned minimized wasted time previously spent fussing with fly changes or clumsily retying a new leader. By the end of the spring, I had probably caught more wild trout than in the past five years combined. From bluelines to bigger rivers, I wielded my new gear with great effect, swashbuckling through pools and runs and racking up impressive numbers of trout. Sure, I still got skunked in tough conditions, or found risers I couldn't fool, or casts I couldn't make. But when I was dialed in, the fish came . . . and came. Gigabytes on my phone were taken up by the same image of my submerged left hand holding yet another trout. Yeah, it was epic.

But here's the thing: it also began to feel a little, I don't know . . . gluttonous. When fish number 8 becomes number 28 and you still want to cast for fish number 48, then wake up in the morning and go for number 58, and then eventually 98, you may have crossed the threshold from gentle sport to the dark side of mindless fish counting.

I noticed something else, too. I started catching the same fish over again. When I scrolled through images of certain trout from certain rivers, I recognized identical spot patterns from fish caught the week before or the previous month. One day I landed a foot-long brown that had my nymph still stuck in its upper jaw from a week earlier—a break off from a doubleheader on a tandem rig (so much for barbless hooks falling out in twenty-four hours). The fish stared back at me from the landing net, now with two Frenchies in its mouth. Its expression seemed to say: "Hey bud, what's your problem?" That's when I also started to feel, if not guilty, then maybe a little silly, all decked out in my angler-ninja gear, hellbent to catch every trout in the river. Twice.

Consider today's astonishing technology available to anglers: 8x fluoro leaders, sunglasses with "sweat management channels," satellites orbiting the earth beaming real-time data of stream levels and water temperatures directly into our phones. Perhaps a thousand years' worth of instructional videos that show every fly ever tied, and every trick, slack-line cast ever thrown are but a URL away. We've got rods with "smooth loading, quick recover action that allow precise accuracy at short distances without sacrificing the power and backbone necessary for punching flies at longer distances through the wind." Hell, if you can't catch a fish with that, better take up pickleball.

So, it's no wonder I hooked fifty trout that day. In all honesty it wasn't that hard, and I'm no Landon Mayer. I was in the right place, the fish were turned on, and I just kept catching them. It was that simple. But it got me thinking about all the other would-be Landons, Leftys, and Aprils out there, not to mention the guides and lodges all putting their sports onto "whacking days" of unlimited hook-ups. And therein lies what could be an epic problem: how many angler-ninjas can a wild trout population take?

Maybe not that many. On my home waters here in the Northeast, some of the trout are starting to look a little beat up—a mangled jaw here, missing scales there. Others seem to fight timidly as if their wildness was broken from that last release, measurement, and photo-op. And these are the survivors. I recently read a stat that said catch-and-release mortality for trout can vary from as little as 1 percent to as much as 20 percent depending on conditions. So, if you whack fifty, anywhere from half a trout to ten wind up as crayfish food. But mortality isn't necessarily measured in the grisly poundage of dead fish on the bottom of a river. Weaken a trout enough through rough handling or multiple releases and it may become a merganser's breakfast. Maybe this is why places like Labrador make you stop fishing for the day after you release three Atlantic salmon (two on some rivers). They don't want you to feed the seals.

So what can we do? No, I'm not expecting us to all turn in our five-weights for five irons and hit the links. But as enlightened anglers, perhaps our goal should be this: use our technically advanced gear, data, and knowledge, and collectively *not* catch so damn many trout. Instead of whacking fifty, throttle back a little. Relax. Breathe. Study the poetry of the river. *Fish* more, but *cast* less. Let's call it a "Slow Fish Movement."

This is tough to imagine, I know. I mean who doesn't want to catch every trout in the pool when the hatch is on, and fish are crushing bugs on the surface? But then I think about the first modern fly angler who landed a big, wild steelhead, considered it for a few moments, and then had the audacity to return it to the river. Alive. Imagine how his fishing buddies must have reacted, each of them probably dragging along a rope stringer of dead fish while they watched. Certainly they were incredulous, maybe outraged, pissed even. But worlds turn on such seemingly small actions. Today, if that same angler intentionally killed a big wild steelie, his friends might toss him in, or have him arrested depending on where it happened.

That same discipline is needed to make a slow fish movement work. Maybe we should take a cue from my friend Dee who, after she releases a nice trout, sits by the water, unpacks a bowl from her sling pack, and smokes. Then she gazes at streamside trees, listens to the gentle hiss of a riffle, or watches clouds float by.

After what seems like a long, luxurious time, she gets up, saunters back into the river, and continues fishing. Her casts—when she makes them—are measured and thoughtful. She treats the stream like a farm-to-table tasting menu, not the all-you-can-eat buffet at Golden Corral.

Another friend told me about his brother who had reached a stage in his fishing evolution when he could stroll to the river with a good bottle of wine and enjoy a glass or two while he watched trout rise. His rod remained at home in its tube. To that I say, *cheers*.

Slow fishing can mean challenging yourself to only go for the best (or hardest) fish. I've been thinking about a well-known pool on the Upper Delaware River. On a typical evening in May or June, maybe fifty sippers come out, and drift boats line up and take shots at them. I've joined the queue from shore and had amazing evenings of multiple releases. Meanwhile, just downstream in a certain tailout away from the fleet, one, maybe two big browns power up from a downstream riffle and gulp mayflies against a grassy bank. When they show—and often they do not—you can hear them sucking down bugs at forty feet. It's a tough drift, but if you fool one, there's a good chance you are about to see your backing. Next spring, I vow to pry myself away from the more reliable sippers for shots at these mighty but mercurial fish. Even if it means that sometimes I may never make a cast.

Here's another idea: ditch the Euronymphing rod for the day and its gillnet efficiency and instead swing some wets. Work on your midge game. Bring binoculars to look for warblers along the stream or watch trout rise. If you've never zoomed in on a mayfly the moment it vanishes into the maw of a big trout, you are missing one of angling's great joys. Plus, you might learn that they are taking number 18 olives, not number 16 sulfurs. Recently, I have taken to fishing enormous hair-wing spiders because violent, water-throwing takes are so much cooler than another ho-hum twitch of my sighter. I know I can probably hook ten on the nymphing rig for every one on the big dry, but who cares?

As I continue to think out ways to personally fish slower, I want to be clear to my fellow anglers: I am not judging; this is a philosophy, not an edict. And to those who have not yet guzzled from the goblet of fifty trout epic days: you should continue to fish hard and achieve that goal—if that's what you're chasing. When you reach that summit, feel free to stroll down the mountain to a gentler river, where some of us former assassin-types will be knee-deep, making slow, full-measured casts, or perhaps none at all.

DUDE, WHERE'S MY HATCH?

TROUT ANGLERS SPEAK REVERENTLY OF THE "EVENING RISE," AN almost mystical phenomenon when a coldwater river shares its living bounty of aquatic insects with the rest of the natural world. Witnessing one unfold like acts in a play—complete with drama, beauty, sex, and death—is one of fly fishing's great spectacles.

It begins when the sun lowers and the sky turns golden. Crepuscular rays catch the transparent wings of mayfly spinners—sulfurs, drakes, March browns—as they dance in courtship overhead. A few golden stoneflies lumber around, splaying their wings before belly flopping onto the stream to force egg sacks below the surface. Squalls of caddis whirl just above the water.

Meanwhile, swallows weave and barrel roll, mouths agape like humpback whales on krill. Warblers, waxwings, and catbirds pick out individual targets. They fly from their perches to intercept the slow and the unlucky. Dragonflies, too, patrol. They lateral into the scrum, grab a mayfly, and leave behind a pair of wings that helicopter downward minus a body.

Cue the trout. The first rises are tentative but slowly build in number and enthusiasm as spent insects hit the water to lay their eggs and die. Casts are made. Flies sucked down. Fish leap. Reels sing. The light dims. Bigger fish enter the stage. Reels soar into arias. Splashes sound more like livestock than trout. Headlamps click on and off as trout are released. Then full darkness sets in, and finally, it ends. Roll credits.

Last June I sat on a favorite rock on my home water on the East Branch of the Delaware River, awaiting this performance to unfold. The setting was perfect; the light softened, the river cool and flowing. Warblers and thrushes sang in anticipation behind me. Except there was one thing missing: bugs. Sure, I saw a few scattered mayflies and some black caddis ghosting just above the surface. But what should have been a cumulonimbus of insect activity was barely a wisp. And yes, a trout rose here and there, and I even managed a regulation East Branch sixteen-inch wild brown on a Sparkle Dun. But something was definitely off.

And this was not the first time. Far from it.

For the past several seasons on a stretch of river that I have intimately fished for more than twenty years, I have noticed a steady decline of hatching aquatic insects. Yes, there are days when bugs still come off and trout rise. And when that happens, all seems right in the world. But more times than not, the consistency and duration of hatches are way down. The three-week Hendrickson emergence has dwindled to a spotty week and a half. March brown mayflies, never overly abundant but predictable and steady, now come off one here, one there. Blizzards of caddis have downgraded to a dusting. Nowadays, I often sit and wait, shoulders slumped, until I eventually skulk back to my car in the darkness, a jilted lover. There are other streams, too, I have noticed. The sulfur hatch on Pennsylvania's Brodhead Creek was once so thick it was nearly impossible to compete with the living mat of naturals coming down the river. It is now sporadic at best, with entire stretches seemingly devoid of these once ubiquitous mayflies.

But maybe it was me, not the bugs. Perhaps I hit several years of bad luck and bad timing on my local streams. The tired fishing cliché is, "You should have been here yesterday." Maybe I should have been here yesterday since 2015. So I posed the question on social media, asking whether other anglers had witnessed a dearth of insect activity. The replies I received were telling.

"Mayfly hatches seem to be way down. When I fished in the '80s with my dad in the Upper Delaware watershed, hatches were like snow. . . . Anecdotal, but I don't see that anymore."

"The anxiously awaited Hendrickson hatch on the Housatonic seems to have faded to near nothing."

Then others seemed to contradict what I was observing, but with caveats: "Solid hatches on Penns Creek all season but old-timers tell me they're not like before . . ."

And finally, a reply from an Environmental Protection Agency (EPA) scientist's personal account summed it up best: "Seems a continent-wide observation, undoubtedly borne out in many waters but coupled with blurry exceptions in others. We don't monitor with precision for these ecologically and culturally important flies to answer basic questions, unfortunately."

The science on the global decline of insects confirms this blurriness. In 2017, a team of German scientists published a jaw-dropping study documenting a 75 percent population crash of insects in local nature reserves. This prompted the *New York Times* to declare in a 2018 headline: "The Insect Apocalypse Is Here." Yet the story goes on to say that much of the evidence lacks baseline data to confirm whether declines are long term or just anomalies. Three years later, a study in the journal *Science* revealed a 9 percent drop in terrestrial insects per decade—but an 11 percent increase in aquatic insects. But this was a "meta-analysis" that reviewed existing studies from around the world rather than conducting its own original field research. The authors said that the growth in aquatic bugs could have been from general trends of cleaner lakes and rivers—or increased nutrient loads related to climate change. Other studies were more definitive, though equally broad in scope. A 2019 paper said that 40 percent of the world's insects could vanish over the next few decades, but it looked at mostly butterflies, moths, bees, dragonflies, and beetles to draw its dire conclusion. Many scientists challenged the results, citing an overall lack of evidence. Then, in 2020, a more specific study in the *Proceedings of the National Academy of Sciences* (*PNAS*) used radar observations to determine that annual *Hexagenia* mayfly swarms in the upper Mississippi and western Lake Erie basins had plummeted by half.

Think of your own backyard growing up, or maybe a place where you camped each summer. Imagine the porch light at your grandmother's house. Remember moths, lightning bugs, or katy-dids? Do you see fewer than you once did? One criterion cited in the *Times* story was the "splatter effect" on windshields from collisions with bugs and how this seems to be lessening. Speaking for myself and using the porch light metric, what once was a maelstrom of bugs swirling around the light at my cabin-in-the-woods in upstate New York has become an anemic whimper in recent years. Large moths—lunas, cecropias, and polyphemuses, once a delightful, several-times-a-summer spectacle, now show up maybe once every other year. Is this peer-reviewed science? No, but it certainly jibes with what entomologists are observing.

No other outdoor pursuit, except maybe amateur beekeeping or butterfly collecting, directly depends upon, reveres, and cele-brates insects like fly fishing. Anglers joyfully geek out on Latin bug names, even creating their own slang: *Isonychia bicolor*, or slate drakes, are "Isos"; the genus *Tricorythodes* becomes "Tricos," or if you are really cool, "Trikes." The aforementioned *Hexagenia* is shortened to the badass-sounding "Hex." I once saw a vanity license plate that read "BAETIS"—the genus for the blue-winged olive mayfly. We tie painstaking imitations of specific life stages of particular aquatic bugs: egg-laying caddis, March brown emergers, crippled sulfur duns. We time vacations around certain hatches on certain rivers. Good luck booking a motel room in the Catskills during "Bug Week" at the end of May when the green drakes are out, or having a pool to yourself on the Madison during the salmonfly hatch. Without healthy, vibrant aquatic insect populations, fly-fishers—particularly trout anglers—might as well take up—gulp—golf.

Let's put fly fishing aside. If you start to pull on the thread of what else relies on aquatic insects, things start to get downright scary. Look around most North American trout rivers during the spring, and the foliage drips with migratory birds hunting and pecking molting mayflies, resting caddis, or stoneflies—not to mention caterpillars, inchworms, aphids, and more. Some migrants have traveled from as far away as the Andes to take advantage of this seasonal bounty. Remove the birds and you have lost a key cog—a natural pest manager and seed disperser. So expect a compromised forest, one more subject to disease and invasive species, and less able to sequester carbon and protect watersheds. Expand the insect decline to things like bees, and you start to lose other ecosystem services like pollination. In other words, a crappy Hendrickson hatch could be the foretelling of something much worse.

So what can we do about it? The truth is that no one really knows precisely what is causing the decline. Still, the widespread use of pesticides is often implicated, along with other factors. The *PNAS* study's authors link the Hexes' disappearance to lower dissolved oxygen levels from warming water due to climate change, plus fertilizer runoff from farms that spawn toxic algae blooms.

You can and should blame big agriculture for pesticides and fertilizers, but also consider your own backyard. In my suburban neighborhood in New Jersey, lawn services lord over the land. Every spring, they dump fertilizers and spray to control "pests" whether weeds or insects (many of which are beneficial). Throw in carbon-spewing two-cycle leaf blowers and military-grade mowers and you have a full-on assault on the landscape. Ironically, many of these same homeowners drive EVs and use solar panels, so there is clearly a disconnect here. By the way, the porch light metric at my suburban house is truly dismal, with just a moth or two and a few errant midges circling even on the muggiest—and presumably buggiest—nights. Not all of us have lawns, but those who do should ditch the lawn service and grab a rake or battery-powered push mower. Or cede (and seed) your lawn with native plants and become more weed tolerant. Dandelions are not the antichrist.

For urban dwellers, buying organic or pesticide-free food would be one way to vote pro-bug with your wallet. And, of course, any chance to reduce one's carbon footprint, including voting for a green agenda, would make a mayfly smile if they had a mouth (adults do not).

Speaking of lights, a 2019 study in the journal *Biological Conservation* noted how artificial lights—everything from streetlights to flaring of gas wells at night—could be laying waste to untold numbers of insects. I wonder if the array of high-powered fluorescent lighting we see around every gas station and strip mall, and increasingly illuminating the outside of suburban homes so you can see them from outer space, are taking their toll. The ones near trout streams suck insects away from more important duties: mating and laying eggs (the *Biological Conservation* study talked about light reflection on roads tricking mayflies into laying eggs on asphalt instead of water). The next morning, dead bugs pile around the light fixtures, the end result of exhausted energy reserves squandered by endlessly circling a 7-Eleven sign. You may not own your own convenience store, but how about flipping those light switches off at home before you go to bed? Or some of us may flip you off.

Is all of this just alarmism from a few fly-fishers crying in their floatant, pining for the good old days? Consider the Neversink. The storied trout river rises in the shadow of Slide Mountain, the Catskills' tallest peak, then wends its way to the Delaware some sixty miles away. Dry fly pioneers Theodore Gordon and Edward Hewitt made their first casts here more than a century ago. It purportedly once supported a green drake hatch, the floppy, jumbo-sized mayfly that famously brings up every trout in the river.

But dams, deforestation, and development apparently took their toll, and the hatch is now functionally extinct. Fish the Neversink in late May or early June, and you might see a handful of green drake spinners, known locally as coffin flies, making their way upriver at dusk, their long white abdomens seeming to glow in the twilight. But they are no longer a true "hatch" with birds, bats, trout, fallfish, spiders, and dragonflies gorging on a healthy river's bounty. The remaining drakes are mere ghosts of what was. Dead bugs flying.

Conservation biologists refer to the "Allee effect" where the health of individuals is directly dependent on the size of the population. Passenger pigeons needed massive numbers—literally billions of individual birds—to survive as a species. When overhunting and clearing of old-growth forests drove numbers below a certain threshold, they went into a decades-long death spiral. The last passenger pigeon, once the most abundant bird in North America and perhaps on the planet, died in a zoo in 1914. Whether some insect hatches, whose strategy also seems to be strength in overwhelming numbers, have already reached that tipping point remains to be seen.

Can humanity turn the insect decline around? Fly anglers are optimistic by nature. Each cast we make is a physical manifestation of hope. We believe that every new fly we tie will be "The One" to surely crack the code. That optimism needs to translate into advocacy or at least personal action to reduce one's own bug-stomping footprint. The same way steelheaders need to be anti-dam, trout anglers should be pro-bug. Let's make "Save the Tricos" trend. As for myself, come next spring, I plan to be back on my rock on the East Branch, ever hopeful the bugs will return. As I said, when the hatches come off, warblers sing, dragonflies buzz, and trout rise, the world is a beautiful place—one worth fighting to protect.

Mountain Badass

New Hampshire's Presidential Range does not rise gently like Vermont's neighboring Green Mountains. Instead, it heaves skyward, raw peaks bursting above the tree line in a defiant jumble of boulders and broken rock.

From this vantage point, where lichens and alpine mosses cling to slabs of granite and mica schist, I stared into misty emptiness near the summit of 5,367-foot Mount Madison. Earlier in the morning, I clambered up a relentlessly steep trail watching clouds lower and visibility dwindle. By the time I reached the final scramble, instead of taking in what should have been a hundred-mile view, I could barely make out scrubby evergreens a couple of hundred yards away. With little chance of the cloud cover lifting anytime soon, I contemplated the three-hour, knee-pounding, four-thousand-vertical-foot grind back to the trailhead. I gulped down some water and began my descent.

The harsh alpine zone gave way to a thick forest of red spruce and stunted birch. Hermit thrushes traded sad songs in the dark woods. My hiking poles clicked away as I navigated rocky scrambles and crossed over rills gurgling from clefts between boulders. In the distance, the sound of rushing water tumbling between mountains faded in and out of range.

Two hours into the hike, gravity eased its grip, and the trail grew more gentle. I continued downward, watching the forest transition to open woods of mature maple and beech. Overhead, red-eyed vireos cheerfully sang "*here I am, over here,*" replacing somber hermit thrushes from up-mountain.

A half mile from the trailhead, I came to a fork marked by a Forest Service sign. One trail led directly to the parking area and my car; the other took a slightly longer route but would wind past a series of waterfalls that I could hear in the distance. Though my legs ached and feet burned, I headed for the falls.

The din of rushing water grew louder. I entered a ravine shaded by hemlock and pine that hugged the stream corridor. Meanwhile, the trail itself transformed from unforgiving rocks and roots to a cushion of evergreen needles that my feet welcomed with each step.

The first falls came into view as a blossom of white hovering beyond dark evergreen branches. The trees abruptly ended, and a narrow thirty-foot plume of water plunged over a rocky precipice lined by mosses and ferns. I followed the trail downhill until the stream dropped another twenty feet, this time over a wide, sloped boulder worn smooth from the endless rush of water. It entered a clear, waist-deep plunge pool in a curtain of spray. Beyond that, the stream hurried into a rapids then fell away once more and out of sight.

I stopped and gazed at the water cascading down. It's all too easy to be mesmerized by a waterfall's obvious raw beauty. Tourists mob them—think Niagara or Yosemite. They've inspired legions of artists from the Hudson River School to Bob Ross. And I get it; they're pretty. But as an angler, I confess that when I see one—particularly on a wild trout stream—I can't help but think about how it might impact fish passage. If it's more than a certain height, I worry it blocks upstream migration and wonder if anything lives upstream. Years ago, in southern Alaska, I learned this lesson first-hand when I fished a gem of a freestone creek flowing through a temperate rainforest complete with hatching caddis bouncing over pellucid pools. It should have been stuffed with coastal cutthroats, but I failed to move a thing. Back at the parking area while breaking down my gear, I spoke with a local picking salmonberries who told me there was a twenty-foot waterfall about a mile downstream. "No fish above it," he said matter-of-factly. A couple of years ago, driving through Jasper National Park in the Canadian Rockies, I learned that many otherwise classic-looking pocket-water brooks dropping through narrow canyons were in fact fishless. Waterfalls again were the culprits.

So, I wrote off this stretch of New Hampshire stream, wild and plummeting dramatically from a wilderness area. I mean, how could any trout possibly exist in such a harsh environment? It was like the evergreens that can't gain root in the boulder fields above tree line because of the relentless wind and cold, not to mention lack of soil.

But then I saw a glint of movement.

Right there, not twenty feet in front of me, holding in the current, swam a wild brook trout. I stood motionless and watched it casually take a nymph in the flow and return to its lie. A few feet farther into the pool, I spotted a second trout finning beneath a fallen hemlock limb. Both fish looked around nine inches long—respectable small stream wild brookies. But how the hell did they get there? There's no way they could have leapt the falls—these were not mighty Atlantic salmon, *Salmo salar*, "the leaper," able to jump waterfalls in a single sweep of the tail. These were brook trout; dainty *Salvelinus fontinalis*, which literally means "little char of springs." Heroic leapers they are not.

And yet, there they were, native trout living their best lives in a foamy pool between otherwise impassable waterfalls, and apparently surviving floods, ice jams, avalanches, and other climactic and geological cataclysms for centuries, perhaps millennia. The brookies' tails wagged in the current, and their outstretched pectorals helped plane the flow. They looked as perfectly adapted to this rugged environment as a snow leopard in the Himalayas.

Then I thought about my own brief experience on this mountainside. Guzzling water supplemented with electrolytes. Wolfing down protein bars. Sweat and pain. It had pretty much kicked my butt.

Back at the car, I peeled off my backpack and finished the last of my water. Then I drove off, leaving the delicate little char of the springs to continue its badass ways swimming between waterfalls, up there in the mountains.

TWO FLIES

THE TWO FLIES STRIKE A POSE. THEY FLIRT. THEY BECKON.

I discovered them in my late friend's tackle collection. Rich was an unabashed fly-fishing hoarder, gifted tier, and amateur angling historian. His cramped apartment resembled a funky, old-school fly shop. Rich had no family. When he died, he left me everything.

When I cleaned the place out, I found correspondence with Lefty Kreh and Joan Wulff. He had original black-and-white photos of tarpon legend Stu Apte and Joe Brooks posing with enormous fish. And then there were flies. Hundreds of flies. Thousands. Everything from impossibly huge bunker patterns to entire dust bunnies of midges. Most of these he tied himself.

But not all of them.

At the bottom of a large Rubbermaid tub stuffed with fly box after fly box was an opaque plastic container the size of a hockey puck. Written in faded Sharpie, the label on the lid read:

E Hewitt
Bi-Vis
Spider

Inside were two flies: a buggy-as-hell size 12 brown Bi-Visible with its signature contrasting white collar, and an elegant badger-colored Spider tied with long, stiff hackle on a size 16 dry fly hook. Could they actually have been tied by Hewitt himself, as the writing on the box indicated?

Edward Ringwood Hewitt (1865–1957) was the Steve Jobs of early twentieth-century fly fishing, and his Big Bend Club on the Neversink River in the Catskill Mountains was Silicon Valley, where his innovations were perfected. He held the first patent on felt-soled wading shoes; he pioneered the use of one-handed rods for salmon—forgoing the bruising, sixteen-foot two-handers preferred by the British; and he was an early authority on stream restoration and trout and salmon propagation.

Hewitt loved attractor patterns and advocated their use. The Bi-Visible—which many say he invented—and the Spider were the Chernobyl Ant and Turk's Tarantula of their time. Hewitt fished these search-and-destroy patterns with deadly effect, twitching and dancing them to provoke awesome strikes. If a trout rose and missed, he would return with a smaller, stealthier pattern to close the deal. To have two classic Hewitt flies would be like owning a baseball signed by Babe Ruth or Lou Gehrig.

I took the flies to a vintage tackle collector's booth at one of the big fly-fishing shows. His eyebrows raised when I presented them, and he studied each pattern under magnifiers for what seemed like a long time. Then he handed them back and told me he was 90 percent certain they were authentic. He said Hewitt had a signature tying style—something to do with how he finished the head—and these two had that provenance.

I asked about value, and he said to the right collector they might be worth around $200.

I took the flies home, not sure what to do. I spoke to non-fishing friends who told me to immediately put them on eBay and cash in. Others said to keep and display them.

But lately I've been thinking that maybe I should fish with them. I know a stretch of the Neversink several miles down-river from Hewitt's long-gone club. It's classic attractor water—tumbling and studded with wheelbarrow-sized boulders. Bubble lines converge at the tailouts. I could picture splattering down the Bi-Visible or twitching the Spider so it stands on its hackles the way Hewitt liked. Big browns would crush them.

What an honor it would be to fish those flies.

Or they could wind up in an overhead branch or bust off on a bad hookset. Then it would seem like an incredible waste.

I take the flies out of their plastic container and stare at them some more. They continue to wink and blow kisses at me.

Trout flies should be cast to trout, right? Help me out here.

One Angler's Junk

God it was ugly.

An ancient fiberglass fly rod leaned awkwardly in the forgotten corner of a vintage/junk shop. It was a seven-footer; clearly home-built by someone either just learning their craft or perhaps giving up on it. Uneven wraps and too few guides clung to a rust-colored blank. A dozen grimy cork rings had started to unglue, losing their noble battle to stay unified as a grip.

I picked up the rod, more as a distraction while my wife ferreted around the shop. It felt light. Surprisingly light. Intrigued, I gave it a tentative false cast. Instead of the expected wobbly, limp-noodle action of junk glass, the rod snapped to attention as if reporting for duty. I false cast again, this time with a little more punch. Catalog clichés of "crisp" and "responsive" flashed in my head. This worst-in-show rod, with its bedraggled guides and free-spinning grip, was, in fact, a lightsaber in disguise. A $79 lightsaber, according to the tag dangling from the off-center stripping guide.

I continued to test-cast the rod. It felt like a five-weight; maybe six. Before my eyes, the dusty junk shop transformed into a tumbling stream. A shelf of antique glass bottles morphed into a bough of rhododendrons leaning over a dark and foamy pool. I pantomimed another cast, shooting twenty-five feet of flyline in slow motion, followed by seven and a half feet of leader and a hair-wing spider. The fly landed surgically, and a heavy brown slashed, hooking itself.

I could hear my wife in the next room negotiating something with the owner. Meanwhile, I had moved on to roll casting Joe Humphreys style, hooking brookies at will.

I took a few quick pictures of the rod and texted them to two friends who immediately began speculating about its provenance. One of them guessed it was a Winston blank built from a kit. The other thought it was a Fisher. "Love the Bakelite reel seat!" one of them wrote. "Offer them $25!" said the other.

My wife emerged from the back room holding a vintage Beastie Boys promotional poster for my son's dorm room. I told her about the rod, and she handed me her change—a couple of twenties.

"Buy it," she said.

I considered the rod with its various warts. I was sure I could talk the owner down to forty bucks—maybe less. Then I would bring it home and restore it to its full glory: new guides; replace the handle with something less bulky, a new set of ferrules—nickel would look nice. Or maybe I would just fish it in its current unwashed form—a way to stick it to Big Tackle and their $1,000 hyper-specialty fly rods, that one designed only to nymph from a boat, this one just to fish with indicators. Fishing with the junk-store rod began to sound very punk.

But then what? Would my punk (or restored) rod join my other vintage glass currently sitting in their rod tubes looking very pretty but doing little else? There's the Phillipson Royal gifted to me by a friend who acquired it from his father-in-law's estate. And the Sila-Flex, with its adorable seahorse logo from Costa Mesa, California, originally owned by the departed uncle of a former coworker. And let's not forget the L.L. Bean Featherweight discovered in what another friend thought was an empty rod tube he found cleaning out a relative's attic. When I opened the tube and showed him the rod, he told me to keep it (he thankfully doesn't fish).

All three rods are lovely, but for the most part, they sit on the bench except for maybe once a year when I decide to play them, taking them out for a few casts, often just on the lawn. I sometimes look at the tubes, crowded among more than a dozen others, and wonder: Just how many rods should one angler own?

I made my decision. With all the self-control I could muster, I took this light-saber-in-disguise, begging to be cast, and put it back in the corner where I found it. Perhaps another angler would discover the rod, take it home, and release its magic. For me, it was unfulfilled love—best to just walk away.

Low Water

The unofficial kickoff to 2024's "Bug Week" in the Catskills came in hot, and I don't mean the fishing. Air temperatures soared to the mid-to-upper eighties, while river temps, at least away from the direct influence of the tailwaters, eventually nudged into the low seventies, virtually shutting down miles of otherwise prime trout water.

Just before the lower mainstem Delaware became too warm to fish, a group of friends and I shoved off in canoes for an annual float/camping/fishing trip. The sun blazed down, so I wore a UV hoodie, long pants, and a buff. The river ran on the low side with a headwind in some spots, so the paddle downriver wound up being kind of a slog (we learned long ago not to bother fly fishing from fully packed canoes). We made it to our campsite in about five hours, stopping once for lunch. Along the way, I thought I was drinking enough water . . .

We offloaded our gear and set up camp. The site, which is on private land owned by a friend, has no direct road access, or nearby houses, or cell service. It's as close to a wilderness experience as one can get on the Upper Delaware, which is why I have camped there since the mid-1990s.

I took a water temperature around 7:00 p.m. Sixty-nine degrees. Damn. My personal cutoff is sixty-eight, and I didn't think it would drop enough by last light, so I decided not to fish, at least for that evening. Instead, I opened a beer and took a comfortable seat around the fire pit. Then I had a second beer with dinner along with some more water—but apparently, not enough.

A little before dark, at what would normally be prime fishing time, one of my friends and I decided to take a short walk to a favorite spot just to see if there were any trout rising or bugs. When we got there, we spotted a few sporadic rises and some sulfurs trickling off, but not nearly the action we would have expected if the river was just a few degrees cooler. On the walk back, we strategized about fishing early the next morning in cooler temps when trout may still be sipping from overnight spinner falls.

We got back to camp, and I sat by the campfire. Suddenly, I began to feel excessively sweaty—so much so, one of my friends asked me if I was okay. I said "yeah" and walked back to my tent, peeled off the UV shirt, and put on a cotton T-shirt. Then I sat back at the campfire. Almost immediately I broke out into a cold sweat and started feeling dizzy. I told the group what was happening, and then said I was going to lie down in my tent for a few minutes. I didn't make it. I walked a few steps before my feet gave out and I found myself sprawled on the ground.

My friends rushed over and asked me what was wrong. I told them I felt lightheaded and just needed to lay there for a few minutes. But then I started vomiting. After a couple of volleys, I felt slightly better, so they helped me back to my tent where I lay there for a while before throwing up some more (thankfully, one of them selflessly brought me his cooking pot, which made a fine receptacle). I started shivering, and dinner and possibly lunch came up again. Then to my horror, I realized it was about to come out the other end. I made it out of my tent, stumbled into some knotweed, and let it fly. I crawled back to the tent. One of the guys tried giving me some water with some electrolyte powder, but it immediately came back up. Now I was scared, wondering what the hell was going on. Was it food poisoning? We all ate the same thing, and everyone else seemed fine. Heart attack? Stroke? The beautiful river and roadless woods now seemed as isolated as deep space.

Lying there in my tent shivering and now cramping up, I considered my options. I called out to the group: "I think I gotta get out of here."

Thankfully, during my puking and shitting, my friends had already discussed a plan. As soon as I made my plea to get off the river, two of them took off into the woods to separate places where they knew they could get a bar or two on their cell phones. They both reached 911, and after some dropped calls and triangulating to determine exactly where we were on the river, a team of EMTs eventually made it to camp on foot. By now, I had pretty much voided my insides, but still felt weak and lightheaded. They helped me to a waiting pick-up truck parked on a rough dirt road. From there, we made our way to the main road where an ambulance waited (they had a helicopter on standby, too, but the EMTs told them to stand down when they could see I was stable).

Inside the ambulance, one of the EMTs (all of whom were amazing) administered an IV along with an antinausea drug that made me feel better within minutes. A half hour later, I was at a local hospital where the medical staff ran some additional tests. It turned out it was dehydration—nothing more. I felt relieved but also a little embarrassed that so much effort had been spent to extract me.

The next morning, I got a ride back to the river and eventually met up with my friends. We decided to break camp early due to the continued hot weather and unfishable river temps, not to mention my health scare. It was the right call.

So, what the hell happened? First of all, and most obviously, I didn't drink enough water. I probably consumed little more than a quart during the float. Twice that would have been more appropriate, and a full gallon a day is recommended when doing moderate exercise (like paddling) in hot weather. In addition, I'm convinced the UV hoodie I wore trapped heat and caused me to sweat even more. I have noticed that some so-called "breathable" fabrics breathe better than others. This one apparently was a dud when it mattered. I tossed it in the garbage when I got home. And of course I could have forsaken the hoodie, buff, and long pants altogether, and worn shorts and a T-shirt slathering myself in sunscreen like the old days.

So, the lesson in this climate-addled future where mid-May is sometimes the new July: drink water, then drink some more. And perhaps swaddling up like a mummy isn't always the best option. And lastly, having trusted fishing buddies who can keep a clear head during an emergency is priceless.

Temperatures have since moderated in the Catskills, and the rivers are cooling again. Time to get back out there for some more swings.

PART IV

SHAD AND FRIENDS

So you'll pretty much fish for anything.

—MY SON, 2018

CASTING FOR *SAPIDISSIMA*

"Too bony . . ." "Cat food . . ." "Bury 'em in the garden . . ." There's a lot of hate out there when it comes to the eating qualities of American shad, the oversized herring that, each spring, runs up the Delaware River to spawn and readily takes a well-presented fly. Ironically, much of this criticism comes from shad anglers themselves, who lob insults at the very fish they have just released. "Cook 'em on a plank, then throw away the fish and eat the plank! Hyar, hyar hyar!"

Lame.

I'm not sure why shad has fallen out of favor as a food fish among anglers. Its Latin name, after all, is *Alosa sapidissima*, which translates to the "most delicious herring." Maybe it's the stigma of the shad's myriad bones—it is ridiculously endowed with one thousand of them, making them the boniest fish in the world. Or perhaps it's the mechanical catch-and-release ethos that has permeated fly-fishing culture. And while I am all for conservation, I am equally in favor of a sustainable, wild-caught meal—particularly one that's guaranteed as good eats by Linnaeus himself.

My fishing pal Jim Leedom and I have been chasing—and eating—American shad on the Delaware River since the late 1980s. We look forward to the annual shad run the same way we would the arrival of any seasonal, local food. A fat springtime shad, properly bled and iced, is as cherished as a quart of wild asparagus harvested from a fallow farm field or a Ziploc bag of morels picked from an ultrasecret woodland (don't even ask).

Come late March or early April, our shad quest begins. I meet Jim at first light in the usual lower river turnoff. We wade to a narrow island then follow a short trail that ends abruptly at a hissing, swirling eddy. Below there, the river regroups then continues along unheeded on its march to the Atlantic. We venture in just knee deep, wary of a steep drop-off and the risk of being swept away. Keeping in mind the brushy island behind me, I roll cast a chartreuse shad fly of my own making on a fast-sinking shooting head. I allow it to settle for a few seconds before stripping it back with sharp jerks. Jim pitches out a shad dart on spinning gear and swings it through the eddy's tailout. Despite our dissimilar techniques, our goal is the same: dinner.

Between casts, we blow on our fingers in the early morning chill. Though it's technically spring, the lower Delaware remains a study of somber grays and browns: the pewter of cold river water, the dark umber of woods still mostly winter-bare. But look closely and there are signs of hope. Some trees are swollen with burgundy buds. Downriver, the first osprey of the year patrols the river channel.

Bang. Shad on. The seven-weight bucks, and a spurt of fly line zips from the reel. Here in this heavy water, the goal is to prevent the fish from powering into the main current and blowing out of the eddy. So I exert as much pressure as ten-pound tippet allows. The fish repeatedly tries to turn into the current, but I won't let it. We play tug-of-war until I can feel the moment when it finally gives up and tacks toward me. I step toward the shore easing it into pebbly shallows. A four-pound female shad, now on its side, repeatedly slaps its tail like a tuna until it beaches itself. It is deep bodied, thick, and as bright as any steelhead. When the light catches it a certain way, iridescent blushes of pink and purple flash back. Just a day or two earlier, this fish abandoned the tide's pull for the first time in three years—since before it entered the sea as a migrating juvenile.

I kneel down and remove the fly. Then I bleed the fish by grabbing its gill rakers and pulling. I turn and see that Jim has hooked up, too, and I watch as he plays his fish the same way—a down-low slugfest. He lands a similar-sized roe, and it meets the same fate as mine. But then the show is over; a fishless hour later, with the sun now over the ridge on the far side of the river, we reel up our lines and decide to call it a morning. One and done—early season shad fishing can be like that. Back at our cars, we carefully place our respective catches in ice-filled coolers. Then we briefly discuss the fine meal that awaits each of our families, and go our separate ways.

At home, the fish is scaled and filleted, and the orange roe sacks carefully removed. Later, my wife, son, and I will feast on broiled shad seasoned with lemon pepper, along with roe cooked on a bed of thick-cut bacon. The fillets have self-basted in their own fat. I squeeze lemon generously on both flesh and roe. Then, using either a fork or fingers, I separate the shad's many bones from its nutty, delicate flesh. Roe, fused with crisp bacon, is piled high. The sounds of lip-smacking and a few low "mmmmms" fill the room. If early spring can be rendered into one glorious feast, we are sitting at the head table.

Three weeks later, and fifty miles upstream, the river valley has transformed into a chartreuse wonderland. River birches and sycamores burst with new foliage. The first migratory songbirds have arrived: phoebes, towhees, yellow-rumped and pine warblers. A fluty-songed oriole zips from branch to branch flashing neon orange. Across the river three hundred yards away, a bald eagle sits low in its massive nest. Fleece hats and fingerless gloves have long been shed and forgotten. But the river itself is still cool, maybe mid-fifties, a perfect temperature for active shad. This spot, a cobble shoal gently giving way to deeper water, suitably lacks the brawling brutality of the lower river.

I stand solo, double-hauling the shooting head. Coils of running line whirl from my stripping basket—essential gear for shad fishing. Then they settle and straighten in the current before I begin retrieving the fly. The key to this fishing is speed—fast, foot-long strips like you were prospecting for bluefish or stripers. The other key is leader length—just two feet of straight ten-pound test and a simple unweighted shad fly—a body of chartreuse ice chenille on a number 8 streamer hook is all you need.

The fly stops mid-strip. Keeping the rod pointed at the strike, I jab back with my line hand. First I feel solid thumping weight, then fly line yanks from my hand and out of the basket. I lift the rod, and the reel shrieks. This is open water, so I give the shad room to fight. It responds in kind with a wild jump and another nice run. It looks to be a male, or buck, of about three pounds. As I bring it closer, a dozen similar-sized shad ghost behind it, curious about its sudden runs and jumps. The hooked fish swims within a few feet of me, prompting the others to peel away two and three at a time. I slide the buck into the shallows and pounce on it.

I clamp the shad to a chain stringer hanging from my wading belt and let it bleed out in the river. But I don't stop casting. Eight releases later, including a fine roe pushing five pounds, it is time to leave. I bring the buck to my car, where another shad angler has parked next to me in his pick-up truck. He looks at the fish, and then at me, and asks with a bemused expression: "You're gonna *eat* that?"

I place the fish in the cooler, taking my time to make sure it is well covered in ice, and then say without looking up, "Oh yeah."

Later, I scale and fillet the fish and then cut it into smaller chunks. I toss these into a container of briny water where they will soak overnight. The next day, I rinse the chunks, pat them dry, and then place them in a jar with alternate layers of sliced onion and carrots, along with a smashed clove of garlic, a bay leaf, and a teaspoon of chopped fresh dill. Lastly, I pour a heated solution of vinegar, sugar, and pickling spices over the fish. I seal the jar and leave it in the refrigerator for three days. On the third day, I drain the vinegar, remove the bay leaf and garlic clove, and replace them with several generous dollops of sour cream. Then I gently stir until the shad and onions are covered. I now have before me the greatest appetizer ever to adorn a crisp flatbread. A tangy, sweet, briny, firm, and creamy gift from the river gods. The traditional accompaniment is a chaser of freezer-cold Scandinavian aquavit, but Absolut over ice works, too, if you must force me.

By the second week in May, I now find myself almost one hundred river miles farther upstream in the Catskills, on the Upper Delaware's famous trout water. It is late morning. And though caddis bounce over rifles and an occasional stately March brown rides the currents, it is shad I still seek. The chartreuse wall of foliage has followed me to this spot, along with what seems like the entire eastern migratory bird population. Vireos, thrushes, tanagers, redstarts, ovenbirds, and other songbirds I can't identify sing all around me. A dark and mysterious pool is a short cast away. Above me, a blue dome with a few lazy cumulus clouds smiles down. I breathe in deep lungfuls of the sweet, earthy aroma of the Delaware River valley in its full spring splendor. At this moment, calf deep, there may be no better place on the planet.

And I am already into a half-dozen shad. A single buck is tethered to my stringer, which I looped around a partially submerged tree limb. By now, my casting has fallen into a pleasant routine. Shoot the line, aiming for the far shore. Let it sink for two seconds, then begin stripping quickly. Repeat until the line jolts to a halt. Strip-set, then let the shad pull the loose line from the basket until it's on the reel.

A drift boat approaches from upriver as I fight another fish. Two sports, both decked out in full wild trout armament, stare at me. They look perplexed at the stripping basket and my otherwise minimalist setup (no vest, landing net, or other high-tech accoutrements; just a fly box, nippers, and leader wheel stuffed in the pouch of my waders). The guide, trying to play it cool as only a fishing guide can, says something about how it's just a shad, and the two sports immediately try to look disinterested. Yet they continue staring as a fat roe damn-near takes me into my backing. They float around the next bend before they can see me land it.

Late that night, I place the shad fillets in a Ziploc bag filled with a solution of water and equal parts kosher salt and sugar. The next morning, I rinse off the brine, blot the fillets with a paper towel, and then let them air dry for an hour. Meanwhile, my trusty Little Chief electric smoker, its insides blackened with a quarter century of sticky tannins and oils, stands at the ready. I plug it in, lay the fillets on the rack, and replace the lid. Then I slide in a panful of wood chips. For shad, I use any wood as long as it's apple. Soon a steady stream of wonderful-smelling smoke trickles from beneath the lid. An hour later, I replace the pan with more chips, and four hours after that, the shad is bronzed with a patina of smoky, caramelized perfection. I will share one fillet with Jim, a surprise for our next fishing trip together. The other one I'm about to devour with my paws like a grizzly bear. I pour myself a chilled mug of spring wheat beer. Then I peel off a piece of shad along the mostly bone-free upper edge. The tang of the apple smoke and the almost creamy flavor of the shad intertwine like two beautifully played musical notes. I sip the cold beer. Then I break off another piece and pick out a prominent Y-bone. I consider it for a few seconds, this quintessential shad calling card, and place it next to the rapidly shrinking fillet.

This will be my last shad of the season. Many have already started spawning, and some of the early fish are past their prime having burned up much of their fat reserves. I'll watch them while I cast for trout at last light. The males torpedoing along the surface chasing females. Later in the summer, pools will dimple with shoals of fingerlings dropping back to the ocean.

Before I know it, both the beer and smoked shad are gone; just an empty mug and pile of oddly shaped bones are all that's left.

The Mid-March Delaware Watershed Slam

EXACTLY ONE DAY AFTER THE IDES OF MARCH, I HIT IT HARD beginning at the Lambertville Wingdam, playing a hunch that early shad may be around. I arrived at the lot at 6:30 in the morning just as another angler pulled in right behind me. We rigged up side by side in the dark, and he mentioned that walleye fishing had been decent. Noted.

When I reached the dam, it looked too high to fish safely, so I set up in the pool below it. The light was still low, so I caved and decided to throw a jig for walleye instead of a dart for shad—at least for a few casts. Sure enough, I had a hit pretty quickly and landed a skinny 'eye. Then two anglers braver than me ventured onto the first part of the dam and began casting plugs. So I joined them, though by now I switched back to a dart as I'll take a mighty shad over a flaccid 'eye any day.

One of the anglers hooked up and fought a fish in the heavy current. He wound up landing a nice 'eye more than three pounds, which he kept. Then it was my turn, but I could feel baby head shakes instead of deep surges of a shad. Another skinny 'eye. A little while later, another. And then something with a little more pull that wound up being about a one-pound smallmouth that decided the dart was food. When I landed it, I realized that I was now halfway to the coveted—but little-known—Mid-March Delaware Watershed Slam (MMDWS). I hooked one more fish that felt shad-like with a brief low-gear run, but then the hook pulled. Damn.

By 9:00, the action died, and some slugabed anglers had joined in, making the dam and adjoining pool kind of crowded. So I left. The night before, I had thrown my trout gear in the car just in case, so I decided to hit a favorite blueline about a half hour north that also happens to be a Delaware tributary.

I parked in the usual spot between the ice cream stand and minigolf course then brewed some coffee on my little camp stove. When the coffee was done, I wandered over to the creek and studied the first pool. A trout rose. Then another. No bugs visible, but cool, cool. Then a few bluebirds landed in a shrub willow in front of me. I watched them just as a pileated woodpecker swooped onto a dead tree behind them on the other side of the creek. Another trout rose. Damn, this may be the best cup of coffee I ever had.

I rigged up and approached the pool. On my first few casts, I swung and missed twice on a CDC caddis emerger. Then I moved upstream and landed my first fish—about a six-inch wild brown. Yes, I made a mental note that I was now three-quarters of the way to the extremely prestigious MMDWS.

I came to another pool with a few risers in a back eddy and landed one of them—maybe seven or eight inches. Then I made a move to the tangled lower stretch that holds the promise of larger fish. Fishing was tough in the bright sun, though; I wound up missing two fish on dries but spooked many more. I also saw some boot tracks, the first time I had come across them in this lower water, confirming that, no, I am not the only human on the planet who fishes this out-of-the-way stream.

Eventually I came to one of the larger pools—a slow run about thirty feet long that allows some rare casting room. When

I approached, I spooked a few smaller fish holding at the tailout. But at the head of the pool, I spotted a nicer trout that apparently hadn't noticed me. I remained still for a while. The fish I had initially spooked seemed to settle down and took up stations in the middle of the run. There was glare where the big fish held, but I could see it make lateral movements in the current—an indication it was taking nymphs. So I opted to fish a dry dropper. I started with an unweighted Pheasant Tail Nymph that went ignored, then switched to a Copper John with the same result.

It was tough getting a drag-free drift, and I knew I was one bad cast away from sending the trout beneath an undercut bank. I switched to a caddis nymph of my own design—just some ice chenille on a weighted scud hook. The cast seemed on the mark, and I told myself to just watch the dropper—don't get distracted looking for the fish to move. The dry eased under the surface, I lifted, and holy crap I hooked it. The trout tried to get to the undercut a few times, but I was able to keep it out of there with rod pressure. It turned out to be my largest ever for the creek—a solid fifteen inches. I released it and moved on to the next pool that had some genuine risers. I caught a few smaller fish there before calling it.

By now it was two o'clock, and I convinced myself that the Delaware had warmed in the afternoon sun and perhaps shad were now active. Plus the glory of the MMDWS hung in the air. So I opted to head back to the wingdam. Surprisingly no anglers were there, so I was able to cast darts unfettered. Pretty soon, I hooked another skinny walleye, then another. And then . . . I hooked something heavier that surged for the bottom. I saw color. Could it be? I hauled it onto the dam, and it was mine. Yes, I had achieved the near-impossible: a Mid-March Delaware Watershed Slam: a walleye, a smallmouth, a wild brown, and the hardest of all: a foul-hooked white sucker, which I now held writhing in my hand.

Shad? Too early . . .

April Madness

You know the scene from the movie *Goodfellas* when Henry Hill snorts several lines of cocaine then needs to sell some guns, pick up his brother, make meatballs, and close a drug deal? Here is my version (and feel free to hum the driving baseline of Harry Nilsson's "Jump into the Fire").

The plan was to hit the Delaware at first light and then maybe a couple of wild streams on my way home but the river was spiking from Thursday's rain so wasn't sure if it would be fishable and didn't want to wake up at 4:30 so I slept in a little and decided to do things in reverse order which meant go trout fishing first then the Delaware later so I packed the car with a five-weight along with my shad rod landing net vest waders lunch cooler and water and headed first to a wild trout stream which I was hoping was running on the high side but it wasn't so I knew the fishing would be tough under bright sunny conditions and it was for the first half hour when I continued to spook trout after trout but then found this one pool where I could see a few risers coming up to midges and I missed one on an RS2 emerger but then the fish stopped rising but I could still see this nice trout at the head of the run feeding on nymphs every few seconds so I retied my leader and began fishing a dry dropper rig making long casts and then finally the little caddis dry dipped under and the fish wallowed for a few seconds then ran directly toward me for a logjam which I assume is its bomb shelter when things get bad so we wrestled for a few seconds with the fish surging to get into the logjam and me not letting it and finally it gave up and I had it in the net a fat fifteen-incher which is a really nice fish for this stream and one of the most satisfying so I left and with my waders still on and headed to another stream but the ice cream stand where I usually park is now open for the season so I had to get my stuff together with all these people watching me while they ate ice cream and eventually I wound up at this brushy pool with some decent trout in it and a few Hendricksons coming off with some fish rising at the head including one nice trout that may have been eighteen inches and it was really hard to get off a cast since this stream is so brushy but somehow I made one and the fly floated tight to an undercut bank and a trout took it then jumped three times and I eventually got it in the net though it wasn't the big one it was still a nice thick trout so then I left to head to the Delaware and walked past the people eating ice cream again and drove to the river but it was really high and looked borderline unfishable but I found a spot on a submerged rock and began casting but caught nothing for the first hour so I looked around and wondered if the fish were pushed right along the shore and out of the current and hell if I was a shad I wouldn't want to fight the current so I began flicking out the dart maybe twenty feet and twitching it back to me and I hooked and dropped a fish then hooked up again and it was a shad so I landed it and put it on my stringer and cast some more then I dropped a bigger fish just before I netted it then decided enough was enough so bought some ice for the fish and headed home and filleted the shad which I will eat for dinner tonight but not before I go clamming this afternoon because the tide is good.

THE BOYS AND BASS OF SUMMER

Summertime, oh, summertime, pattern of life indelible, the fade-proof lake, the woods unshatterable, the pasture with the sweet-fern and the juniper forever and ever, summer without end.
— E. B. WHITE, "ONCE MORE TO THE LAKE"

"I'M NOT OBSESSED WITH FISHING LIKE YOU ARE, DAD," MY SON, Finn, often tells me. And he is right. Unlike his father, Finn chooses not to rise at four in the morning to chase a tide. And he definitely does not linger on a trout river well past dark wiping no-see-ums from his arms by the dozen while waiting for mayflies to hit the water. My own father, born and raised in New York City hard by the banks of the East River, is a fully citified non-angler. Perhaps fish-obsession, like they say with musical talent, skips a generation.

But for one glorious week each summer, Finn joins me in a fourteen-foot skiff on a place called Newboro Lake in southern Ontario where my wife's family has owned a cottage since the 1980s. Here, for seven delicious days without Wi-Fi, Finn's Xbox controller is exchanged for a light spinning outfit, and *Fortnite*

Battle Royale means chasing the evening smallmouth bite with his dad.

Fishing on this lake is refreshingly low tech—at least how I approach it. No fish finders or other electronics clutter the boat. Our trolling motor is a creaky set of ancient wooden oars, the tips of which are slowly turning to compost. We triangulate using a faded paper depth chart, glancing at landmarks while casting to rocky points or the edges of deep weedbeds. The only luxury is a new twenty-horsepower four-stroke Mercury with a push-button electric starter. My father-in-law bought it when the original outboard finally died after more than three decades of honorable service.

Newboro is part of a chain of lakes that links the St. Lawrence to Ottawa through a series of canals constructed after the War of 1812. Forward-thinking Canadians felt they needed a navigable waterway to fight off any future invasion by the Americans. Today, birds and fish, not warships, lord over Newboro's quiet waters. Osprey and Caspian terns patrol overhead, great blue herons stalk the shallows, and loons steam through its bays. Beneath the lake's forty-five hundred acres, bass, pike, and various panfish are found off its lightly peopled shorelines and scattered islands, many of which remain uninhabited.

I take care with my son not to be an obsessive Ahab about fishing here. True, the evening last-light session is sacrosanct; but daytime is often spent swimming, motoring to a local "jumping rock," or otherwise loafing. Sometimes I'll take a few casts off the dock with the two-weight fly rod I bring along and raise bluegills and pumpkinseeds to a tiny cork panfish popper. And if we do fish for bass during the day, it often includes a side trip where we tie up at the local marina and get ice cream. It's summertime, after all; success doesn't need to be measured purely by fish landed.

After dinner, with bathing suits and wet towels hanging from the porch railing, things start to get more serious. Each night, I sit in the boat and ritualistically prepare tackle before we head out.

I rig a half dozen rods with an eclectic mix of lures—some old, some fresh out of the package. During the seven-hour car ride north, we make a traditional stop at a well-stocked tackle shop just before we cross the Canadian border. I always imagine the owners high-fiving each other when they see me drive up. With credit card in hand, I inevitably fall for the latest bass fishing trend. One year it was tube jigs—strange squid-like lures with dangling tentacles. I bought them by the handful. Then came salted plastic worms fished "wacky style," where the hook is hung dead center allowing each end to slowly undulate (a surprisingly deadly technique). This year I fell hard for a new type of minnow plug purportedly developed by fanatical Japanese bass anglers. It came with small "finely tuned" spinners fore and aft, and, according to the box, "catches neutral, suspended fish." They had me at "catches."

But I fish timeless standbys, too: I wouldn't leave the dock without a Zara Spook, a classic surface lure that made its debut in 1939. Two years ago, I landed a pair of four-and-a-half-pound smallmouth—twenty-one-inch tanks—on a frog-colored Spook. Since then, I carpet bomb entire bays and coves with this exact lure hoping to recapture past glory. And at least one rod is always rigged with the same type of curly-tailed jig I began fishing with when I was Finn's age. Sometimes, if it's a windless night, my eight-weight fly rod is in the mix strung with a deer-hair bass bug or Clouser Minnow.

With rods readied, I start the motor. Finn knows the routine. He follows the narrow path leading to the dock, undoes the cleat hitch he had been practicing for the past few days, and steps into the boat.

We motor along while I run the highlight reel of the past several days through my head. There was the pike Finn hooked on a rubber worm that surged for the bottom repeatedly before finally yielding. It measured two feet long—certainly not large by pike standards, but nearly as big as Finn's smile when he landed it. Two nights ago, he boated a black crappie as big around as a hubcap. The night before that, the smallies briefly turned on and Finn hung a solid two-and-a-half-pounder that took line in spurts, then unleashed an end-over-end leap like a landlocked salmon before eventually coming to the net. There were giant pump-kinseeds lit up like billfish that covered an outstretched hand; hit-and-quit rock bass that would crash the lure mightily then do little more than wiggle before giving up. Then there was the unseen fish Finn fought for a while before it eventually powered into a weedbed and broke off. Was it a five-pound largemouth? An eight-pound pike?

For me, this would be the year of "the gift." Finn found the lure the other morning stuck on a rope hanging off one of the floating docks and presented it to me. Perhaps a bass fisherman working the shoreline snagged and broke it off. It was a beat-up black rubber worm threaded onto a plain jig head. But it looked fishy as hell, so I rigged it to a four-and-a-half-foot ultralight spinning rod spooled with four-pound line, thinking it might work for panfish. That night, smallmouth repeatedly walloped it, bending the little rod at impossible angles and making the toy-sized reel chatter away. I finally lost it when I was releasing another bass and left the lure dangling off the side of the boat. A crazed smallie came up, grabbed it, and then jumped ripping the worm off the hook. Whoever, or whatever, left that black-tailed talisman on the dock has my sincerest gratitude.

I ease the throttle and shut off the motor. Finn and I both start casting. Loons yodel across the lake. Caspian terns gracefully fly about looking for baitfish pushed to the surface. Somewhere in the swamps behind us, we hear a colony of herons emitting crazy shrieks that make us laugh. We speculate what they might be saying to each other and agree that it must have something to do with fish. The western sky begins its evening light show with the sun dropping behind low clouds now haloed in orange and purple.

We drift past a rockpile. I miss a hard strike on a jig then briefly hook something that tears off line before shaking free. Finn hooks what at first he thinks is a weed, but it turns out to be a big smallmouth that rockets out of the water just feet off the boat before throwing the lure. He looks at me, mouth agape and smiling, and makes another cast. I quickly switch to my trusty Zara Spook and miss a solid blowup. On the next cast, a big bass takes hard then leaps, shaking its head and rattling the lure. Finn grabs the net and scoops it up. Three pounds easy.

We make another drift. By now Finn has switched to a Spook. Two large bass crash the surface near his lure but don't connect. One of the fish looks truly enormous, and we marvel at the crater it leaves behind on the lake's surface. Then, just like that, the fish turn off, just as the first mosquitos of the night begin buzzing us.

The few clouds on the horizon have now darkened. The sky quickly fades from cobalt to charcoal. Saturn already shines down along with a few early stars. We turn on the running lights and begin to head back to the cottage. I know Finn is happy with the evening's action—he hooked a good smallmouth, helped me land a nice fat bass, and saw a few other big fish come up. He won't pine over lost fish or missed opportunities like his obsessive father might. I tell him on the boat ride back to remember this evening when it's the middle of winter and he has algebra homework or a test the next day.

Because however unending and sweet summertime fishing may seem, it inevitably does come to an end.

Bass in the Nick of Time

"Just give me one good hour," a charter boat captain from Montauk used to say, claiming that sixty minutes of prime fishing time was all he needed to make a day on the water worthwhile.

But what if you only have a half hour to begin with? How much good fishing would make the trip a success? These were the questions that gnawed at me as I stood on the dock of my in-laws' cottage in southern Ontario. Dinner would be served in thirty minutes. "Stay out as late as you want," my mother-in-law had told me, but I knew I should be back by 7:00.

Across the lake, in a quiet cove, where a rocky shoreline dropped off into dark and mysterious water, a loon's gentle yodel beckoned me like a siren's song. My watch read 6:35. A few wispy clouds on the horizon had already begun to turn gold in the soft evening light. The loon called again. Now it was 6:36. I grabbed my tackle—an ultralight spinning rod and a handful of lures—slid them behind the seat of my kayak, then shoved off and began the five-minute paddle to the other side of the lake.

As I glided along, a dragonfly kept pace with the kayak the way a dolphin rides the bow wave of a cruise ship. Two other boats drifted outside of the cove; one was a sparkling red bass boat, dripping with a full complement of fishfinders, trolling motors, and other gadgetry. The other was a posh pontoon boat—a virtual floating living room, complete with couches and swivel seats. My little kayak, scarcely more than a slab of molded plastic, and barely longer than I am tall, suddenly seemed decidedly low tech.

On the other hand, kayaks allow anglers to slide in quietly among feeding fish. They are also light enough so that a large, or even not-so-large, fish can tow it around for surprising distances. Still fresh in my mind was the fifteen-pound striped bass that took me on a miniature Nantucket sleigh ride around Sandy Hook Bay last fall.

I stopped paddling and let the wind push me silently into the cove. Dense beds of milfoil, elodea, and other aquatic weeds rose just under the surface. While such areas make great hiding spots for baitfish and aquatic insects, predators—bass and pike—prefer the edges, where they can dart out and ambush prey.

Eventually, the weedbed dropped off, revealing the brown skeletons of a few fallen trees scattered on the bottom. Forgoing the new bass lures I had just bought, I tied on an old favorite: a black marabou jig with paint chipping off the head. Earlier in the week, I stocked up on a battery of plugs, spinners, even something called a "salt-impregnated tube-jig" that the guy in the tackle shop assured me would get the big one. In the water, however, it looked like a hot dog with a hook in it and had about as much appeal to the fish.

I cast the lure beyond the submerged trees and began twitching the marabou jig, trying to imitate a crayfish or a leech swimming among the branches. My line suddenly tightened. Snag. The snag shook its head. Fish. Line peeled off the ultralight reel, and the kayak began pivoting in the direction my rod was pointed. Nice fish.

A husky largemouth bass cleared the water in the kind of gill-rattling leap straight from the cover of an old *Field and Stream*. It crashed back into the lake, jumped again, then dove under the kayak, forcing me to pass the rod over my head to keep the line from rubbing against the hull.

After a few more runs, the fish surrendered, allowing me to grab it by the lower lip. Eighteen inches, I guessed, maybe three pounds. I let it go and began casting again. Another fish grabbed the jig and began taking line, spinning the kayak in the opposite direction. The line rose, and a similar-sized largemouth leaped just off the bow, splashing me with warm water. The fish headed for the bottom, and I held the rod high to keep it from the safety of the dead trees.

The fish eventually relented to the little rod and, like the one before it, came in quietly. I admired the jagged black line that ran down its flanks, and the deep potbelly that good-sized bass so often have. Giving the fish one last look, I twisted the jig free, and watched it sink out of sight.

By now, a chorus of bullfrogs had begun their baritone calls near some distant lily pads, and the first of the evening's mosquitoes buzzed around my head. In the fading evening light, the lights of the cottage twinkled through the branches of birch trees. I turned the bow toward them and began paddling. My watch may have said I still had time, but it turned out that ten good minutes was all I needed.

THE FISH OF
FORTY-THREE CASTS

As ANGLERS, WE'VE ALL HAD THOSE MOMENTS WHEN WELL-meaning—but non-fishing—friends try to set you up to fish with someone they perceive as a fellow angler. "You should meet my brother-in-law," they say. "He *loves* fishing!" Then you find out the brother-in-law likes to soak chicken livers for bullheads with a boom box and a thirty-pack. You bring the thirty-pack.

So, when I ran into a buddy who told me about his coworker who was a "serious fisherman," I was dubious. That is, until he said: "I think all he fishes for are muskies." *Muskies*? Muskellunge? The fish of ten thousand casts? The one that eats ducks and musk-rats and two-pound suckers? The mythical fish that I have never even seen, let alone caught? I immediately asked if I could go ahead and text him. He said he'd check and let me know.

A few days later, I got the green light to reach out and so I did. Then I got a call. His name was Jeff, and yes, he was a self-professed muskellunge addict. He told me how he plans vacations and takes days off around certain moon phases when muskies are most active. This guy was serious. We set a date to meet at a lake the following week.

When I hung up, I added his contact to my phone: "MUSKIE JEFF."

The next week, I met Muskie Jeff at the launch ramp of a fifty-acre impoundment in New Jersey stocked with muskie fingerlings years ago that now naturally reproduce. Jeff said local panfish anglers now complain because their catches have dwindled while fifty-inch muskellunge gorge on bluegills and crappie like popcorn.

He splashed his boat, and I climbed aboard. A battery of heavy bait casting outfits lay on the deck, some retrofitted with strange, oversized trigger grips reminding me of a cache of bazookas. Next to the console, hundreds of plugs hung from dairy crates lined with rows of plastic inserts—oversized jerkbaits, glidebaits, and crankbaits, along with massive cartoonish soft plastics that looked like something out of the *Star Wars* bar scene except for the 7/0 treble hooks hanging from them.

But even with this arsenal of gear, I had read enough about muskies to know that the odds of actually hooking one were slim. Unlike trout or stripers that spend much of their time feeding or searching for food, muskies, for the most part, are loafers. They suspend off a weedbed or drop-off for days before finally deciding to scarf down a single large meal—maybe a keeper largemouth or a bullfrog the size of a softball. After it eats, it sinks to the bottom next to a fallen tree and becomes a logjam potato for the rest of the week. The windows when they actively feed have Powerball-like infrequency. Hence the whole ten thousand casts thing.

The first thing Muskie Jeff did was take a lap around the lake trolling plugs, which he explained can yield the rare aggressive fish. It didn't. So we moved to the edge of a weedbed and began casting. Jeff used a foot-long jerkbait. I tried one of the bazooka baitcasters rigged with a soft plastic called a "Husky Medusa"—a fifteen-inch, nine-and-a-half-ounce leviathan with three thick curly tails, cartoonish googly eyes, and a dinosaur back. What it imitates, I have no idea, and I don't think I want to know.

Using the rod like a trebuchet, I reared back and launched the flailing mass of tails and hooks into the lake where it crashed down like a dead mallard. Subtle fishing, this was not. I cast and pumped the lure back to the boat maybe a dozen times. But I found the rig overpowering, so I swapped it with a heavy spinning rod. Jeff handed me a jerkbait, which I attached to an eighty-pound leader, and I began ripping it though weedbeds.

And then . . . on what was definitely more than my thirtieth cast, but less than my fiftieth, the lure yanked back. I set and saw a yard-long tannish flash.

I. Hooked. A. Muskellunge.

The fish ran toward the boat then dove deep, and I had to plunge the rod into the water to keep the line from fouling in the stern. Before I knew it, Muskie Jeff lowered a massive landing net and scooped up my unicorn. Thirty-seven inches long and thick, we estimated it might push fifteen pounds. After some quick photos, I held the fish in the lake by the tail before it swam off. Afterward, I sat for a while, beaming. I had just hit the Powerball.

But since this was muskie fishing, a long period of self-flagellation followed. We spent the rest of the day bombarding the lake, swapping out lure after lure, with not even a follow or swirl to show for our efforts. At the end of the day with the sun setting, I asked Muskie Jeff something I had been thinking about all day: what was his average catch rate? He looked at the darkening sky and considered the question. Then he said that with good conditions like we had today, with two guys fishing hard like we did, he would expect to catch . . . nothing, not a thing.

So, that's muskie fishing. I may quit while I am way, way ahead, though I keep thinking about that one-in-ten-thousandth cast, the one when that huge, audacious plug you're ripping through the weeds stops . . . dead.

Anglers of Winter, Chisel in Hand

When autumn fishing winds down, most anglers hang up their tackle, winterize their boats, and begin their annual hibernation from outdoor pursuits. But for others, the long wait is nearly over, as they eagerly ready their toothpick rods and toy-sized reels. For they are members of the small, but fanatical, sect who jig through the ice for panfish—bluegills, crappies, and yellow perch. They are the jiggermen.

Warm-weather anglers pine through the winter months, gazing forlornly through frost-covered glasses, while jiggermen cheer on Alberta clippers and hoot and holler as the mercury rattles around the ball of the thermometer like a frozen pea. They gather at tackle shops and have meaningful debates on the merits of tipping one's jigs with either waxworms or mousies—a type of fly larvae (read: maggot).

One winter, however, the wait was interminable for most jiggermen, myself included. Blame it on El Niño or climate change, but most lakes in the Northeast remained ice free for the entire season. I remember watching the Weather Channel and tracking polar air masses, only to watch them fizzle out somewhere over the Great Lakes. The sled I had rigged for ice fishing, complete with rod holders, a bucket for sitting, and even a space for my thermos, remained by the back door like an anxious puppy waiting to be let outside. By mid-January, it was covered with dust instead of snow or ice.

Yet I did manage one ice fishing trip at the end of that long, warm winter, and it turned out to be worth the wait. My friend John McMurray called me in early March with an invitation to fish a private pond in southern Massachusetts. I half thought he was joking, but he promised that it not only had adequate ice from a cold snap a week earlier, but it also contained some of the largest yellow perch he had ever seen. This was all the prompting I needed.

Jumbo yellow perch—called jackperch or cows—are the jiggermen's most prized catch. Forget pickerel as long as your arm, forget giant largemouth bass whose bloated bellies barely fit through the ice hole. To a jiggerman, a fourteen-inch-jackperch with black eyes, orange fins, and a humped back streaked with deep olive bars is as good as it gets.

But it must be caught on a jigging rod the size and strength of a twig, and a tiny reel spooled with two-pound line. Then it should be filleted—preferably with several of its friends—dipped in egg, dredged in panko breadcrumbs, and fried until it turns golden brown and crunchy. Leave the bass for humid summer evenings and popping bugs, the pickerel for weedy bays and streamers.

When I joined John on the pond that miraculous day, it was as if I had stumbled onto a scene straight out of Currier and Ives. John and his friend Ted Williams stood sentinel over carefully chopped ice holes. Already a few perch lay scattered on the ice, some well over a pound and a half. A light snow fell, as if sent down by Old Man Winter himself, dusting the boughs of a few white pines on the far side of the pond.

Ted is a hard-core jiggerman and ice fishing purist. He proudly uses a homemade ice chisel to chop holes, shunning conventional augers. He mostly fishes with a Swedish Pimple—a lure that's to ice fishing and perch what the Adams is to trout streams and brookies. He sweetens the end of his hooks with the eye of a perch, claiming that the scent triggers reluctant cow-perch into biting.

Ted hooked a particularly big perch while I readied my tackle. "There's another," he called out, snapping the rod upward. Then, like a bear swatting a salmon from a stream, he snatched the fish from the hole. "That's a cow," he said, holding the nearly two-pound fish.

By then, I had threaded a wax worm onto my jig, and lowered it to the bottom. I then began the ever-so-gentle jigging action that triggers perch into mouthing the lure. A fly-fisherman might boast that a trout sipping a spinner is the most subtle take in all of angling. But compared with a perch inhaling a jig below the ice, trout feed with all the finesse of a blue marlin smashing a trolled bonito. At best, perch hits are barely perceptible—the line may quiver once, or go slack, or slowly inch to one side of the hole. Sometimes the rod tip hiccups a fraction of an inch.

I lightly jigged the rod again, felt a slight increase in weight, and lifted. The rod jerked downward, thumping in time to the head shakes of a nice perch. Then the fish ran and line spun off the reel. I quickly dropped the rod tip into the water to prevent line from chafing on a sharp edge in the ice. A few seconds later, the head of a jumbo perch poked into the hole. I reached in, grabbed the fish around the midsection, and flipped it onto the ice. The jackperch stared blankly, its dark sides and orange fins contrasting sharply with the newly fallen snow. Taking Ted's cue, I quickly snapped its back and placed it on the ice, where it lay still.

For the rest of the day, the fishing continued at a slow pick. Mixed in with the perch were several two-pound largemouth bass and a few nice-sized pickerel—prized any other time but, on the hardwater, little more than unwanted thugs that we quickly released.

At last light, four more perch came up over a ten-minute period, including two that pushed fifteen inches. Finally, at dark the action shut down completely. With snow continuing to fall, we gathered up around a dozen jackperch from the ice—not a huge catch, but a welcome respite from an otherwise ice-free winter, which, to jiggermen, can be particularly long and cruel.

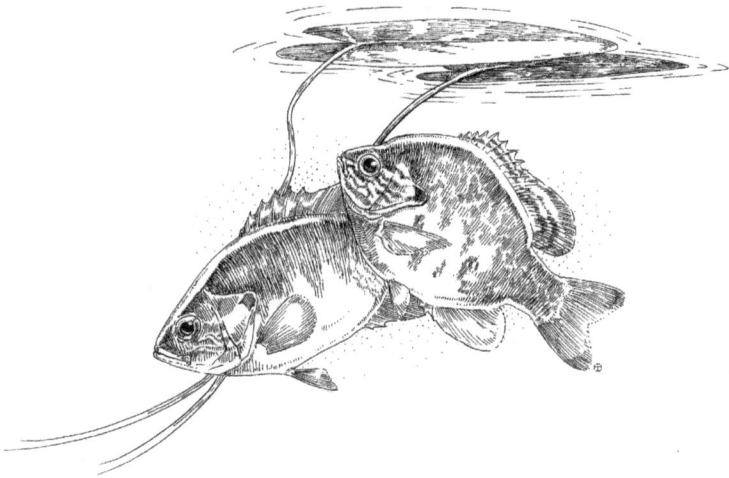

PART V

SALTY

What does the tide have to do with missing your cousin's wedding?
—My mom, 1997

WAITING FOR ALBERT

ALBERT IS LATE THIS MORNING.

I sit on a salt-bleached log worn smooth from wind and tide, staring out at the flat-calm Atlantic. My stripping basket, buckled around my waist, rests in my lap. My nine-foot eight-weight sits in the cradle molded into the rim of the basket. Intermediate line is carefully wound in loose coils. A 1/0 Surf Candy, loop-knotted to fifteen-pound fluorocarbon, sticks from the cork of the rod grip.

I am so totally ready.

Except, where is Albert?

Every September, from New Jersey to Nantucket, they arrive. Call them Fat Alberts, albies, false albacore, little tunny, *Euthynnus alletteratus*—whatever you'd like. They come when the first big cold front of the season flushes baitfish out of estuaries. They swoop in like squadrons of strafing P-51s, swashbuckling in a ballet of carnage. Silversides, bay anchovies, and sand eels shower in flight. Tunny stylishly leap after them, their emerald backs gleaming in the sun. They are audacious, these scale-model tuna, abandoning their pelagic home each autumn to gorge within a roll cast of the beach.

That is, when they feel like it. Oftentimes they do not, which leaves shoals of wader-clad fly-fishers restlessly standing around sandy points or inlets, waiting. Some clutch flies between thumb and forefinger like an addict's last cigarette. Their eyes constantly dart about looking for anything that could indicate the slightest possibility of a fish—a hovering tern, a dimple behind a wave. They seem to be in a perpetual state of distraction, but in reality they are as focused as an astrophysicist contemplating string theory.

You can catch many more albacore from a boat, no question about it. Anglers chase down surfacing schools then drift into them from upwind. They sometimes hook doubles or triples, then do strange dances around and around as they fight their fish. Then they chase down another school and hook some more. One fish blurs into another. Catching an albacore from the beach, on the other hand, is beautifully inefficient. It's like skating flies for steelhead instead of dredging with lead. Both techniques work; but you remember the single fish that came to the dry far more than the six you took down deep.

I remain seated on the log. The early autumn sun feels good on my face. A flock of sanderlings have alighted twenty feet away. They scurry to the sea's edge, then come rushing back just ahead of the next wave. Don't they ever get swamped? I look beyond them but all I see is an empty ocean.

Yes, Albert certainly is late this morning.

Sometimes, though, he is early. Annoyingly so.

His premature arrival usually comes by way of a report posted on a local surf fishing forum. It seems to always happen on a Tuesday or Wednesday when most of us are busy earning a living. Guys with handles like "SurfNut55" or "AlbieAddict38" (or is it 39?) will gush: "*Epic* today. Fish busting everywhere!!! Arms killing me!!!"

Don't these people work?

By the time I show up Saturday morning along with the rest of humanity, it's blowing snot out of the Northeast. And Albert has retreated to the twenty fathom contour to gorge on butterfish.

Damn you, Albert.

Even when Albert is on time, he can be fussy. There have been moments when I have stripped the most perfectly presented fly directly through two dozen gorging, slashing, marauding tunny and nothing happens. It's hard not to take up golf after this. On a warm morning last fall along the New Jersey shore, I watched for the better part of a tide while albacore boiled and porpoised almost nonchalantly in and out of the surfline. Over a couple of hours, three out of fifty anglers hooked up, random as lottery winners. Then I peered below the surface and could see the problem: thousands—make that millions—of half-inch fry hurrying along. God knows what they were, young-of-the-year bay anchovies? Juvenile sand eels? A size 14 Pheasant Tail Nymph would have been too big. Eventually the school moved on and I went home, arms killing me, but for all the wrong reasons.

Other times, it's a distance thing. Last year (again!), I watched the surf turn purple as large numbers of hickory shad pushed a massive school of rainbait into a rip. It was a stunning sight: the white blossoms of busting shad erupting on dark undulating clouds of baitfish, with delicate terns hovering then diving into the melee. But the albacore stayed back, content to occasionally rip the surface seventy-five yards out. A ten-knot headwind quartering in from the east further handicapped me. I grunted and groaned and double-hauled as best I could. Each time, the fly landed impotently maybe sixty feet away. Then a surfcaster strolled up next to me, nodded, and cracked off a rifle shot with his eleven-foot rod and Van Staal reel. His lure—a two-ounce pink epoxy jig—went impossibly far. He cranked twice, then lurched back and hooked an albacore.

Freaking Albert.

Virtually every albie I see landed is mechanically released. Anglers revive the fish by thrusting them headfirst into the water. This jump-starts them back to life, and they swim off stiffly wagging their tail like a wind-up toy. I release mine, too. Well, most of them, anyway. There's a myth that false albacore are an inedible, foul, bloody mess. Pure hokum. The trick is to bleed the fish immediately, then gut it and pack the body cavity with ice. This cools down the endothermic muscle unique to tunas that enables super-fast bursts of speed. The muscle also gives off heat, which can spoil the flesh.

At home, I fillet the fish then cut out the center blood line. This leaves four crimson-colored loins. You can slice the meat very thin and serve it raw with ginger, wasabi, and soy sauce. Or cut the fillets into chunks and toss them in a marinade of soy sauce, white wine, ginger, olive oil, garlic, and dry mustard seed. Let it sit for an hour or two, then sear it on the grill leaving it rare in the middle. A beach-caught albacore served this way with sweet corn on the side, or maybe sliced Jersey tomatoes and fresh basil drizzled with oil and vinegar, makes for a fine autumn harvest. Pair it with a hearty Oktoberfest beer and all is well with the world.

From the perch of my log, I glance behind me—briefly, of course—and see bird activity in the bayberry shrubs on this rare-as-gold undeveloped New Jersey beach. The birds are small and hyperactive, darting from branch to branch feeding. These "LBJs" (little brown jobs)—probably fall warblers—are now olive drab, having shed their springtime breeding plumage and song. One time while waiting for Albert to show, I heard a muffled thud and then squawking overhead. I looked up to see two peregrine falcons following an injured shorebird one of them had just struck. It spiraled into the ocean and crash-landed just beyond the waves. The peregrines swooped repeatedly over the floundering bird seemingly unsure what to do. Perhaps they were juveniles and had not learned the fine art of administering the final coup de grâce to their prey. Just then, an adult black-backed gull that had been loafing on the beach casually took off, landed next to the shorebird, and ate it headfirst. I was as stunned as the peregrines.

I have seen other things, too. The spouting humpback whale perfectly silhouetted against an orange sun that had just risen above the horizon moments earlier. The snapper bluefish driving onto the sand thousands of young-of-the-year fellow bluefish. The nude sunbathers strolling past me, waving. Sometimes, whether or not Albert shows up feels irrelevant.

Oh, but when he does . . .

I sometimes hear them first. It sounds like a group of teenagers having a splash fight in a pool. Then they erupt in front of me, lunging through the waves. I'll have four seconds to get off a cast. Haul once, then shoot. Tuck the rod and strip back fast. Don't set the hook until you feel the full weight of the fish, even if you see one streak in and crush the fly. Otherwise you may pull it out of its mouth. I did this three years ago on a beach in Rhode Island, and it still haunts me. When the line comes tight, strip set, then watch fly line jump from the basket. Then: backing, glorious snow-white backing. Yards and yards of it dump off the reel into the Atlantic. After that, things you rarely experience: the very real thought you might actually get spooled; the strange whining noise that backing makes when fully stretched; hand cramps. Eventually you back up and the ocean presents to you one of its lords. False albacore look like something imagined by Da Vinci—the ideal of the perfect fish. The high dorsal that folds into a slot and completely vanishes. The recessed panels where each pectoral fits perfectly. The scimitar tail. The swatch of blue green camouflage along its back. The large, ever-eager eye. All elegantly designed for high speed and pursuit.

I take in a deep lungful of salt air and exhale slowly. I unhook the fly from the cork and hold it between my fingers. It feels better there. I gaze at the ocean, ever-patient, waiting for Albert.

THE SURFMEN OF MONTAUK

They say Montauk's blitzes have gone away with the tides. That the acres of frothing stripers that once rounded the point—seemingly on a daily basis just a few years ago—are now just a fading memory. With them have gone the internet heroes—the GoPro-wearing YouTubers, the Instagram influencers, the cell phone junkies looking for the sugar high of a fish on every cast. They have wheeled away like a flock of restless gulls now setting up in places like the Cape Cod Canal or some other latest hotspot where fishing for "large" is currently "epic."

But still standing along Montauk's rocky shores and sandy beaches are the keepers of the old guard. They vary in age. Some have faces chiseled and furrowed from season after season of wind and waves and salt. Others are fresh faced and eager. All have eyes that belie secrets: starry bass-filled nights, or the heart-break of a parted line or bent hook and something unmention-able forever lost.

They are mostly solitary, these anglers. You may find them perched on crusted boulders with white water creaming all around. They fire out cast after cast. The cleats of their boots stand in the same footsteps worn smooth from decades of anglers who came before them. Other times they walk past, silent and ghost-like, heading out as darkness descends. Their rods hang over their shoulders like weaponry. They don full wetsuits or waders with foul weather tops cinched tight. They wear military-style belts with gaffs, pliers, and knives secured to them. They look as ready to battle with the elements as with fish. Yet it's the less tangible opponent: fatigue, loneliness, boredom, or lack of confidence that often proves most formidable.

True surfmen know failure. They often cast from muscle memory alone. They think of the thirty-pounder that slammed a bucktail next to a particular outcrop a decade ago, or the savage blow-up on a pencil popper made from an immense fish that never came back. Maybe this time it will. They rotate their go-to lures: battered swimmers, needlefish, darters.

And just often enough, they are rewarded. Knees bend, a rod lurches seaward, and a reel's drag yields yards of line. A bass is landed. The fish may be released or kept. Watch them handle their catch and there is little wasted motion. Look closely and you may see their default thousand-yard stare replaced by an expression best described as reaffirmation.

And then they cast again. All Montauk surfmen have one thing in common. They are relentless. They cast and hope. Cast and hope.

QUEENS BLUEFISH
ARE KINGS

THE PROMISE OF HUNGRY STRIPED BASS SHINED AS BRIGHT AS
the nearly full moon rising in the early evening haze over Long
Island. Though not a swirl or splash could yet be seen, Rob Maass
and John Waldman stood supremely confident, casting bucktails
from shore into a quiet backwater.

They had lured me here with tales of wild fishing they had
stumbled upon only two days earlier. Between them, they landed
nearly sixty fish, all stripers in the range of three to six pounds.
They told me how the bass had pinned schools of spearing against
the shoreline, gulping them down by the dozen and swiping at
nearly any lure tossed their way.

What made the invitation even more tempting was the oddball location: an utterly urbanized shoreline of Queens, along
a dead-end cove of western Long Island Sound. Directions
included parking near some garden apartments, then wandering
under a highway overpass while keeping a low profile so as not
to tip off any potential commuter/anglers as they zipped home.
Catching a fish under such conditions seemed downright illicit—
in a playing hooky sort of way.

More than anyone I know, John and Rob have assembled a formidable cache of equally funky spots. John, a former scientist for the Hudson River Foundation, chronicled New York Harbor's prolific wildlife in his book, *Heartbeats in the Muck*. Maass once spent two years filming anglers in New York City for a documentary on the subject called *Gotham Fish Tales*. The two have even wet their lines in the Gowanus Canal in Brooklyn, which John describes as "punched senseless by man." Even there, they have caught fish.

Perhaps a trip to the Gowanus was now in order as the three of us continued to cast with no results. Rob theorized that the tide may be to blame, since it would flood nearly two hours later than the other night. John, on the other hand, silently fired cast after cast into the cove until, finally, he yielded two small stripers around fourteen inches each.

In the meantime, I had switched to a surface popper, if for no other reason than to watch it slowly chug along the glassy surface of the cove. With a light spinning rod and six-pound line I brought to match up with the schoolie bass, I could send the weighted lure a couple of hundred feet.

As the popper began another slow, gurgling retrieve, a large swirl appeared behind it. I thought for a moment that a striper may be following, when all at once the lure and everything around it seemed to explode in a wild shower of spray. I lifted the rod and a hundred feet of line poured off my reel, the telltale sign of a big bluefish. The fish stopped, briefly shook its head and stripped off another hundred feet for good measure.

Now, clutching a deeply bent fishing rod that seemed as inadequate as a stick and some old string, I remembered that John and Rob had warned me that a few large blues had been patrolling the cove, probably in pursuit of the small stripers. Hooking into one on such light tackle, and the brawl that would surely follow, must have seemed foolhardy enough that I had blocked it out of my mind.

Meanwhile, the fish held deep, shaking its head repeatedly like a dog that refuses to give up its favorite sock. Tremors shot up the line, down the rod, and into my upper arms. Large blues, with their sickle-shaped tails and thick, muscular bodies, can do this indefinitely it seems.

And so it went for the next ten minutes. The bluefish would sometimes turn, if only for a moment, allowing me to gobble a few yards of line back on the reel, only to resume its head-shaking routine once more. At one point, the fish came halfway out of the water, its gaping mouth looked as if it could chomp a small striper clean in half.

By now John and Rob had wandered over. I continued to draw the fish closer with my strained rod. Finally, I steered it into the shallows, where it kicked its tail one last time and beached itself.

On the shore lay a bluefish that John estimated at thirty-six inches and easily fourteen pounds. I slipped the barbless popper from its huge mouth, then grabbed it by its tail and slipped my other hand under its prodigious belly to hold up for a photo. But the big blue would have none of it. It wrestled from my grip and thrashed back into the water, pushing a torpedo wake as it sped away.

No more big blues came that night. And though the stripers never did show up either, by the next day a satisfying twinge of stiffness had settled into both arms.

WE'LL ALWAYS
HAVE HERRING

WHEN STRIPED BASS FINALLY CLEARED OUT OF LOCAL WATERS shortly after New Year's Day—marking the end of the latest migration in recent memory—they left behind vast schools of sea herring. For weeks, the bass had relentlessly gorged on the herring schools both inshore and offshore. But eventually, water temperatures dropped enough to send the last of the stripers to points south, or to their wintering grounds up the Hudson River.

When that happened, most anglers broke down their rods, rinsed and oiled their reels, and, like the bass, began a three-month hibernation until the waters warmed again in late March.

Others, however, decided to go herring fishing.

Considered to be among the world's most important food fish, sea herring range throughout the Atlantic from North Carolina to Norway and are caught commercially by the tens of millions. Young herring are canned and sold as sardines; larger fish are salted or pickled. The fish's iridescent scales have been used in paint and to make faux pearls.

Bigelow and Schroeder's seminal *Fishes of the Gulf of Maine*, originally published in 1925 and still ranked as perhaps the greatest of all references on marine fish, dedicates some thirteen pages to sea herring. Atlantic salmon merit only eleven pages. Further, the authors, who frequently deviate from straight science-speak into lyrical prose, confess that "herring fresh from the water are among the most delicious of our fishes."

Apparently many still agree, as reports of anglers lined shoulder-to-shoulder along piers, jetties, and bulkheads began to emanate from local tackle shops.

Which is why Dery Bennett and I decided to meet at a New Jersey beachfront. The day before, I had spotted four fishermen perched at the end of a jetty, flipping small silvery fish out of the water, two at a time. When I approached them, silvery scales could be seen covering the rocks like newly fallen snowflakes. Periodically, one of the anglers would grunt and send another volley of shimmering fish up over his head and onto the jetty. One of the others would immediately drop his own rod, unhook the fish, and toss it into a bucket. When I peeked inside, dozens of herring up to a foot long stared back.

But as Dery and I strung up our light spinning tackle, conditions had changed from the day before. A strong cold front had roared through overnight, dropping temperatures twenty degrees. To make matters worse, a gale-force wind screamed down the beach.

Not surprisingly, the jetty was desolate, except for a few black-backed gulls, hunkered down and looking miserable. We plodded to the end of the jetty anyway, trying to keep our multihooked herring rigs from tangling in the wind.

At one point, a particularly strong gust blew the lid off my bucket, which I had to chase down like a man chasing after his fedora. Eventually, we found level rocks to stand on, and, despite the wind, both of us managed to get off decent casts.

When my rig hit the water, I let it settle for a few seconds, then began retrieving it in twitches and jerks. To my surprise, almost immediately I felt a little flurry at the end of my line. I continued to reel. The weight suddenly seemed to increase, and my rod-tip danced and twitched with each crank. A few seconds later, I found myself grunting as I jerked a brace of silvery herring out of the water and onto the rocks. When I glanced at Dery, he too was hauling up a fish.

I briefly examined one of the herring before I slipped it into the bucket. At first glance, it seemed rather plain, almost like a fish a child would draw with a string of bubbles coming out of its mouth. But upon closer examination, its subtleties became more apparent. Like a shad, its mouth was underslung and scooped, perfect for gobbling up small shrimp and other crustaceans. Its deeply forked tail indicated that it was always on the move.

Bigelow and Schroeder captured the beauty of the herring's colors when they described the fish as "[d]eep steel blue or green-ish blue on the back with green reflections . . . indeed fish just out of the water are iridescent all over with different hues of blue, green and violet."

For the next hour, the fishing continued fast and furious. Doubleheaders, tripleheaders, even a handful quadruple hookups that had us laughing as we tried to lift our own personal school of fish out of the water.

Some herring jumped like scale-model tarpon. Others ran deep and tried to tangle your rig in the rocks. If more than one fish was hooked, an organized run by all of them would peel a few feet of line from the reel.

Eventually, the five-gallon bucket I had brought began to fill, and Dery reminded me that each fish would have to be filleted, as per the pickling recipes we both planned on using. As it stood, we were each looking at a couple of hours of scaling and filleting.

So, with untold thousands of hungry fish only a short cast from where we stood, we left. As the shoals of herring had done with striped bass more than a month earlier, the little silvery fish had outlasted even us.

THE SURF KINGS OF
THE JERSEY SHORE

NORTHERN KINGFISH LARGELY DISAPPEARED FROM OUR WATERS
by the mid-1960s, and with them went a whole culture of summertime surfcasters who would fill seaweed-lined baskets and
steel pails with the delicious "kingies."

Also known as king whiting or surf king, the fish still evokes
faded, black-and-white images of cigar-chewing fishermen clad
in porkpie hats, long khaki pants, and madras camp shirts. But
now the kingfish seems to be making a comeback in parts of its
range, particularly along the Jersey Shore.

I figured it was my turn to catch a "nice mess" of fish. I packed
my gear and headed down the Garden State Parkway for the
historic kingfish grounds. Brigantine Island just north of Atlantic City seemed like a perfect spot, since it was a favorite of the
mighty Van Campen Heilner, who pioneered surf fishing there in
the 1920s and 1930s.

Brigantine lies east of Grassy, Little, and Reedy Bays and a
maze of endless meadows of spartina grass and tidal creeks. In the
summer, the spartina takes on a soft green color, salted with the
occasional whiteness of a stalking egret, and the creeks and bays
are gray-blue.

When I arrived on Brigantine, a light fog had rolled in, brought in by a cool, onshore breeze. Atlantic City was mercifully no longer visible. I walked to the Absecon Inlet jetty through the fog, and as it slowly came into view, silhouettes of fishing rods could be seen poking out from every direction. As I got closer still, between fifty and sixty anglers were now visible, covering the one-hundred-yard jetty. My pace automatically quickened, knowing that thick crowds usually mean fast fishing.

The farther out on the jetty I walked, the more serious the fishermen became, until I finally approached a group of five who were stoic. They fished in perfect synchronization as only seasoned fishing partners can. They shared the same jetty rocks and silently passed bloodworms to each other. One would duck as the other cast. All eyes were intent on the water. These were the kingfishermen I hoped I would find.

Just then, a hook was set, a rod quivered, and a fourteen-inch kingfish was yanked from the water, unhooked and slipped into a large spackle bucket, all with mechanical efficiency. As casually as I could, I wandered over to the bucket and peeked inside. It was full of kingies.

I stumbled over to the next available rock and strung up my rod. Another fish came in, and another. I managed to tie on a kingfish rig—a stiff leader with two hooks looped on—followed by an ounce-and-a-half sinker. I dodged a bloodworm's pinchers and halved it, threading each piece on a hook. I tossed the rig out with my light spinning rod, felt it thud on the bottom, and waited.

My eyes turned back to the kingfish masters. An angler who looked around seventy was their obvious leader. He sat on a canvas foldup stool as the others stood, and he fished a beautiful custom conventional rod, as the others used spinning tackle. I watched as he reeled slowly and carefully, crawling and hopping his rig along the bottom, eyes fixed on the rod tip. He then stopped and leaned forward, extending his arms. A quick wrist snap sent his rod into a beautiful arc. He reeled steadily now, the rod dancing and shaking.

He snapped his wrist again and swung a double-header of glistening silver kingfish out of the water and onto the rocks. The stoic look was now replaced with a big smile that showed teeth like Dr. Seuss's Grinch, and his entourage erupted into laughter, whoops, and hollers. This was not his first double.

Bump, bump, bump, and I was in, too. Kingfish take a bait like their cousin, the weakfish. It's a lunch-on-the-run grab that could send your tackle into the depths if you put it down for the wrong second. They fight as hard as any fourteen-inch fish has a right to, with plenty of little head shakes and dives for the bottom.

I pumped the fish to the surface and lifted my first-ever surf king onto the jetty. The fifty-degree water made the fish feel ice cold in my hands. The kingfish's underslung mouth, where the hook and bloodworm now dangled, reminded me of a redfish, and its faint vertical bars were perch-like. But the dorsal fin is what really sets the kingfish apart. The first ray extends inches above the rest like a feathered plume, giving the fish, if not a royal appearance, then at least a classy one. I placed the kingfish in a bucket, where it beat out a rapid-fire rhythm with its tail.

Six other kingfish joined it that day—a far cry from the kingfish masters who caught no fewer than one hundred between them—but still filling my category of "nice mess." Before leaving, I overheard a kingfish recipe given by one of the masters: roll it in corn meal and fry it in bacon grease. Amen.

HOLY MACKEREL, IT'S ANOTHER HERRING

Twin diesel engines growled as we passed the sea buoy off Shark River Inlet, some thirty miles south of downtown Manhattan. The eighty-foot party boat, packed to the gunnels with an eclectic array of tackle and salty fishermen, headed due east to deep ocean waters. For my then ten-year-old nephew, Johnny, the long wait was over.

I once offhandedly mentioned to Johnny that the surest way to catch lots of fish was to sail aboard one of the many party fishing boats out of Sheepshead Bay or the Jersey Shore. He stood wide-eyed, as if I had just uttered an eleventh commandment. "When can we go?" he asked.

So I considered the possibilities. In my teenage years, I would go on all-night bluefishing boats whenever I could save enough money for the fare. But a ten-pound bluefish, with its savage runs and sharp teeth, seemed like too much for a fourth-grader. Additionally, bluefish boats can quickly devolve into scrums of anglers tangling lines and yelling at one another—all in the name of good fun, of course.

Then reports began trickling in that the mackerel run had started. Mackerel arrive in vast schools, and when the run hits its peak, they can be hauled in three and four at a time on multihook rigs. Although they fight hard for their size, they average only about a pound each. And they are truly beautiful fish, with sleek silvery bodies and a greenish "worm track" running along their backs, reminiscent of brook trout. They seemed like the perfect fish for a kid (or grownup).

Johnny and I wandered around the deck of the party boat, taking in the funky atmosphere that occurs only when seventy strangers go fishing together. At the bow, three anglers swapped their favorite hunting tips, including how to climb inside a deer carcass in a blizzard ("Don't rupture the gut sack or it stinks"). The stern seemed to be reserved for heavy smokers, except for one steely-eyed old salt gazing at the horizon intently, perhaps still looking for U-boats.

Inside, the crowded cabin had the feel of a subway car, with roaring engines drowning out most conversation. One man read a newspaper, looking every bit the part of a commuter on his way to the office—except for his knee-high rubber boots. A father and two sons devoured hard-boiled eggs bulging from a large Ziploc bag.

The captain eased the throttle, sending the passengers into something that resembled general quarters on a battleship. Anglers dashed madly out of the cabin and onto the deck. Rods were lowered as if they were oars on a Viking longboat heading into battle.

Johnny and I took our spots at the rail. When the captain tooted the horn, we dropped our rigs to the bottom and began jigging our rods in an attempt to attract mackerel. Almost immediately, an angler next to me set the hook. A few moments later, a shimmering two-pound mackerel came sailing over the rail, then quickly went into a large cooler.

We waited for our turn. Johnny had the fixed gaze of a red-tailed hawk staring down a rabbit hole. But nothing happened.

After ten more minutes, the captain blew the horn again, and we reeled up our lines to find a new spot.

To pass the time, and to hide my eroding confidence, I pointed out a gannet. Immense white birds, gannets hunt by plunging into the water beak first from a hundred feet and higher. A few minutes later, Johnny began spotting them on his own, proudly calling out birds over the roar of the engines.

The captain slowed the boat again, and we lowered our rigs. This time, something latched onto my line almost immediately. I glanced over, and Johnny had a fish on, too. Based on his expression, it could have been a thousand-pound swordfish.

We lifted shimmering sea herring into the boat. Herring schools often run with mackerel, though they are considerably smaller, with most barely reaching three-quarters of a pound. I glanced around wondering if we should throw the fish back or keep them.

"I'll take 'em for cod bait," said the angler who caught the mackerel, opening his cooler. "Toss them in here."

So now we had a purpose: to fill a cooler with herring. We lowered our rigs and immediately hooked up again. Throughout the boat, silvery herring were now flying over the rails.

And so it went into the afternoon, with Johnny catching herring two, three, and even four at a time. Eventually I stopped fishing and simply watched as he landed his fish, threw them in the cooler, then wiped fish slime on his jacket.

Finally, the captain tooted the horn three times, then fired up the big diesels. It was time to head back to the dock. Anglers reeled up their lines, some grumbling about how few mackerel they caught. I felt disappointed, too, and was about to give Johnny the requisite "we'll get 'em next time" speech.

Then it occurred to me that to a ten-year-old who had never been deep-sea fishing, a herring-is-a-mackerel-is-a-bluefish-is-a-blue-marlin. He didn't care what he caught as long as it had scales and tugged on his line. So I proudly declared that we had had an excellent day of fishing. And I meant it.

Johnny leaned against the rail of the boat in a contented haze. His jacket was now a medley of slime, fish blood, and dozens of herring scales. He filled his lungs with salt air, tinged with diesel fumes.

Then he asked, "When can we go again?"

BACK IN BLOCK

BLOCK ISLAND. THE REMOTE NEW ENGLAND OUTPOST LOCATED some twelve miles at sea—a place where rugged surfcasters heave enormous lures into surging waves, where tales of fifty-pound striped bass hang in the air like salt spray crashing over its rocky shore. This is not one of those stories.

Since 2005, a group of a dozen anglers, including me, has descended onto "Block" every September for a weeklong gathering known as StriperKamp. We board ferries and private boats and head due south from Point Judith, Rhode Island. Some have traveled from as far away as Alaska and Hawaii. We rent a large house and for a week live like Vikings, venturing to sea and then gathering each evening to eat, drink, and regale.

Our group represents walks of life as diverse as our fishing techniques. Among us are seventy-something Vietnam vets, twenty-something software engineers, waterfowl biologists, dock builders, and fisheries managers. There are trollers, jiggers, eel slingers, plug chuckers, spearfishers, and bait drowners.

And one serious fly-fisher. That's me.

Block Island is small, less than ten square miles. But among striper fishermen, its fishing provenance looms like Everest. During the early to mid-1980s, large bass—true giants, with some weighing more than sixty pounds—would stage every November off its rocky points. Mere thirty-five-pounders were sneered at by locals and dubbed "Block Island schoolies." Plugs like the needlefish, which imitates the large sand eels bass gorge on, were perfected here. Eventually these huge fish mostly vanished, the last of the great year classes born in the late 1950s and 1960s. Today, with few exceptions, all that's left from those glory days are faded Kodachromes and a few skin mounts of bass the size of third-graders gathering dust in bars and basements.

But that was all plug and bait fishing. In all the accounts I have read about those magical few years, there is nary a mention of a double haul or a Deceiver. Admittedly, Block is not set up for fly fishing, unlike its more famous neighbor Martha's Vineyard, which lies some fifty miles to the east. The much larger Vineyard is blessed with many salt ponds, cuts, and gentle beaches, which are perfect for fly casting. Block, on the other hand, consists mostly of rock-studded shorelines blasted by relentless creaming waves. It's a place where hard-core surfcasters look and say, "Oh yeah," while most fly-fishers say, "Oh crap."

But there are places to punch a fly if you know where to look. And if solitude outweighs hard poundage of fish, you've come to the right place—particularly if you venture out after the summertime tourist crowds dissipate.

Each year, the few fly-friendly spots shift like Block's restless shorelines. Last fall, on the island's normally placid western side, I found a cobble bar awash with white water from a distant tropical storm. Though it was midday and under a bright sun, the spot— no bigger than a large trout pool—erupted with breaking bass whenever a large wave broke. You would wait for a series of rollers to pass, and behind them, bass up to twenty-eight inches long would charge in, chasing silversides and other baitfish right at your feet. My plug casting friends watched with envy as I matched the hatch perfectly with a size 1/0 Surf Candy and hooked three fish to their one. The fishing lasted for three delicious days, ending when the storm finally spiraled away.

Other times, in a place known locally as the Coast Guard Channel, where Block's lone salt pond drains, schools of false albacore streak through bait schools, guns blazing, sending anglers running to and fro like Keystone Cops. But those albie runs are notoriously mercurial, and more times than not, you stand around like a wallflower waiting for a dance partner who never shows up. Still at other times and in other places, toothy bluefish viciously grab streamers intended for bass, surprising me with their savagery and tail-walking leaps.

Schoolies dominated our most recent trip—meaning striped bass from eighteen to twenty-four inches. But what they lacked in heft, they made up for in sheer numbers and aggression. Nearly all my shore-bound fishing friends, regardless of where and how they fished, racked up large numbers of them.

For me, it would be the year that stripers briefly morphed into brook trout. I discovered this phenomenon on the first night of our trip. The evening began with the usual StriperKamp over-the-top feast, starting with appetizers of smoked salmon, jumbo shrimp, dry salami, and assorted cheeses. Then came lamb chops, cooked rare along with string beans from a Kamper's vegetable garden, followed by heaping dishes of warm apple pie, all chased with a dram or two of single malt. Afterward, I reluctantly pried myself from a table filled with fishing friends and the kind of laughter and conversation that comes only after a truly great meal, and stepped into the night air.

The moon, now two days off the full, rose over the island while I quietly pulled on waders, strung my eight-weight, and clipped the belt of my stripping basket around my waist. With bursts of laughter emanating from the house's open windows, I followed a path through a bramble that led to the salt pond. The path continued to a low marsh, and I squished through a wet meadow that ended at a series of grassy islands that in turn opened up into the pond itself. The silhouettes of moored sailboats stood ghostly a few hundred yards away. On the far shore, I saw the twinkle of lights from distant houses.

At first, I mistook the slapping sound for breaking waves on a nearby shoreline. But on this still, nearly windless night, the pond remained glassy calm. The slaps turned out to be bass, dozens of them chasing peanut bunker in less than a foot of water. With the marsh behind me draining with the ebbing tide, stripers had set up on a broad flat, where they strafed fleeing bunker schools at will.

Over the years, I have seen and heard plenty of bass on tidal flats chasing bait, but never so many and in water so skinny as on this night. And as it turned out, never were they so willing to take my fly. I started out with an old Farnsworth Fly—a type of balsawood slider—that came from a late friend's fly collection. On a steady V-waking retrieve, a bass crashed it, missing several times before finally gulping it down nearly off my rod tip. In water little more than a foot deep, the fish ran particularly hard, briefly spooking several others cruising nearby. A minute or two later, it came to hand, a perfectly proportioned twenty-two-incher.

Bass continued to gorge, and my fly rarely traveled more than a yard or two without at least a miss or a swirl, and more usually a solid wallop. A half dozen quickly came to hand. Eventually, when the fly began to lose its charm, a quick change to a Tabory Snake Fly prompted more strikes on nearly every cast.

It was nothing less than magical out there. The fishing had an intimacy that transcended the brutality that can typify saltwater fly fishing: grunting double hauls into twenty-five-knot gales, finger-burning runs, and fish so powerful, you are almost scared to wrestle a fly from gaping jaws. Instead, this shallow nighttime bay became as intimate as a native trout stream. The spartina grasses could have been rhododendrons, whistling oystercatchers singing warblers, and the silvery September moonlight the late evening sun of June. And the bass, with their pen-and-ink stripes, looked as beautiful as native brookies. It was a glorious place where the size of the fish truly became irrelevant. And all the while, with our rental house no more than a few hundred yards away, I still heard an occasional eruption of laughter—a sort of chorus to the joyful drama of fish and tide playing out in front of me.

Eventually the fishing slowed, and the house grew silent. By the time I walked up the path, well past midnight, with a baker's dozen bass released and twice as many hooked or missed, all I could hear was the breaking surf somewhere in the distance.

The fishing continued like this for the next few days. Each morning, our group would go their separate ways—the boat guys jigged delicious sea bass and scup off deepwater ledges; the surf-casters found more bass and some enormous bluefish on topwater plugs. Even a few false albacore came to a lucky few throwing metal.

Then after another fine dinner, and warmed by a finger or two of brown liquid, I would join the bass again as they chased bait across the flats. Eventually some of our group tagged along with me, dusting off the fly rods they sneaked along "just in case." We all caught fish.

On our last full day, I found myself casting alone once again. This time I fished until last light and watched scattered bass schools erupting here and there under hovering gulls. Most were well out of casting range. I knew in a few hours, when the tide dropped, they would stage once again in the shallows where I could reach them. But I decided to leave them alone. I reeled in and headed to the house for laughter, food, and drink. The celebration continued long into the night, under the waning moon, surrounded by feeding bass and Block's rushing tides.

BLOCK AND BLUE

ONE FALL A FEW YEARS AGO, STRIPERS PULLED A NO-SHOW FOR the annual weeklong trip to Block Island. By day 3, it became apparent that bass were not in their usual nighttime lies in any numbers (part of a troubling coastwide trend). So we faced two choices: cry in our beer, or pull on our big-boy waders and enter the scrum known as daytime surfcasting for bluefish.

We chose wisely.

In the early 1980s, when striper populations were crashing up and down the East Coast, blues rushed in to fill the breech. They saved the charter industry, which switched to trolling umbrella rigs and wire line for "gorilla blues." Surfcasters adapted, too, though some scorned bluefish as "stinkfish" and "yellow-eyed devils" that destroyed lures and live baits or bit through their leaders with their powerful teeth. They kicked the fish back into the surf or sometimes threw them onto the beach, leaving them to rot. Even today, this stigma continues. But with striper numbers dropping, I suspect we may have to lean on these underrated and disrespected gamefish to once again save the day.

An ebbing tide hurries blue-green water over a long bar of cobble. Waves collide and recede, and golf-ball-sized rocks click and clack around our boots—sand in the making. Ten- and eleven-foot surf rods load and launch, sending pencil poppers, little necks, and giant Docs seaward.

We work the lures back to the beach, each angler fishing to his own cadence. Some reach high up the rod to make it rhythmically pulse back and forth; others stoically reel and pump, reel and pump. A crater opens in the ocean, and something enormous takes a lure. A rod bends deeply, and the angler walks the hooked fish well away from the group to allow the others to continue casting. Then, in slow motion, a blockish head, mouth agape, followed by fourteen pounds of blue-gray muscle, tail-walks sloppily over the waves. A few of us cheer. Some root for the angler, others for the fish.

After what feels like a long time, a thick-shouldered, thirty-five-inch bluefish slides onto the beach, still gnawing on the lure like a pit bull refusing to give up a hambone. Pliers are unholstered, the hook twists free, and the fish slides back into the Atlantic.

If bluefish have one fault, it is their overeagerness to destroy anything that moves. And while hooking fish on every cast may sound fun, it quickly devolves into the mundane. On this day, however, the blues remain delightfully selective, with a fish raised—and often missed—on every few casts. Each individual blowup, each hooked fish, each head-shaking leap is a singular event seared into the brain.

I fight a very large blue for nearly ten minutes. It destroyed a Doc—a nine-inch surface walker that prompts napalm-like strikes. The fish has powered deep into the rip, where it tacks against a three-knot current. When I finally coax it to the lip of the beach, I see it in the clear water—a yard's worth of bluefish with a smaller fish ghosting behind. Just then, the lure yanks free. The smaller blue immediately grabs it, jumps, and throws the Doc nearly at my feet. I chuckle, shake out a few hand cramps and fire out another cast.

Rob Maass's beached fish lurches unexpectedly and tears an errant treble across his finger. Blood spills on his waders and the still-flopping fish. He eventually releases it and sucks on his finger. The bumper sticker "Give Blood, Play Rugby" flashes in my mind, except this one says: "Give Blood, Go Bluefishing."

The fishing begins to slow with the slackening tide, and I put the word out to the group to please keep the next fish they land.

The ever-spiteful Fishing Gods must have overheard me because the action immediately falls off a cliff. Casts become more frantic. Paul hooks up, and I plead with him not to lose it. A few minutes later, a thirteen-pounder flops onto the beach. Like a grizzly, I pounce on the pretty fish. (Yes, bluefish, with their trim lines and blue-green backs, can sometimes be pretty.) I quickly bleed it on the beach, then walk it to the truck. Back at our house, I carve off two thick fillets, which I skin, cut into thirds, place into Ziploc bags, and refrigerate.

I have big plans for this fish.

A couple of hours later, I take out the thickest shoulder meat, slice it thin, and pile it onto a plate alongside some pickled ginger, a dollop of wasabi, and a bowl of soy sauce. I present it to the group as sashimi, and they surround it like tuna on a bait ball. The shoulder meat has a creaminess to it and none of the fishy taste that is too often negatively associated with bluefish. Immediate bleeding and chilling is everything.

The next two pieces, also thinly sliced, have been marinating in a mixture of lemon and lime juice, finely chopped red and yellow pepper, red onion, and cilantro, along with olive oil and a dash of fiery Thai chili paste. I serve it in a large bowl with corn chips on the side. An authentic ceviche—bright and colorful, washed down with various lagers, Belgian ales, and a hefeweizen or two—quickly vanishes.

The following day I serve the last two pieces, but only after I brined them for a few hours and placed them in the electric smoker I lugged along on the ferry. They puff away, and eventually emerge, bronzed and with a darkened rind along their edges. I fold them into a bowl with a brick of softened cream cheese, chopped shallots, and lemon juice. After the flavors have married for an hour or so, I serve applewood smoked bluefish pâté with stoneground wheat crackers.

This gladiator of a fish has been duly respected.

Block Seals and
a Surfcaster's Lament

Block Island's North Rip surges and churns today just as it has for millennia. Swells from the Atlantic face off against the tides of Block Island Sound, skirmishing along a mile-long sandbar that eventually drops away into 120-foot depths.

For surfcasters, this is hallowed ground. Where the bar rises to meet land at Sandy Point, a washing machine of whitewater creates the perfect hunting ground. Bass, bluefish, false albacore, and bonito patrol the drop-offs preying on baitfish disoriented by this upwelling of currents. Heave a big popper or tin into these waters, or double haul a Clouser, and hang on to your cork.

Except now, it is unfishable.

Sure, you can still make the long walk over cobble and sand, past the stately granite North Lighthouse, and stare in awe at the foamy rip and hissing breakers that beckon you to cast. But know you will not be alone. Chances are, about one hundred seals will watch your every move.

For the past few decades, seal numbers have dramatically risen throughout coastal New England and points south. A 2019 federal study noted that numbers of gray seals at haul-out sites more than doubled from 2005 to 2015. Cape Cod alone now supports between thirty thousand and fifty thousand of them. On Block Island, we began to notice grays more regularly around 2010 along with harbor seals, and their numbers continue to grow each year.

In some ways, the return of seals is one of the great American conservation stories of the past half century. A combination of bounty hunting (Maine and Massachusetts once paid out $5 for each seal killed), and entanglement in commercial fishing nets drove numbers to near extinction in U.S. waters by the early 1960s. Then passage of the Marine Mammal Protection Act in 1972 safeguarded all seal species, along with whales and porpoises. Seals responded in kind and began recolonizing from Canada and northern Maine, slowly spreading south. Today, they are routinely found well into New Jersey and even haul out on beaches and rockpiles in New York City's five boroughs.

But with breeding success come growing pains, and anglers now find themselves in conflict with a fellow fisher that outguns them in every way. Gray seals can swim more than twenty miles per hour and can dive to fifteen hundred feet. The big males, nicknamed "horseheads," weigh up to nine hundred pounds and reach ten feet in length. All come equipped with a mouthful of teeth designed to grab and shred. Even their molars are fanged. Your Van Staal is not competing with that.

Consider what happened a few years ago at Block's North Rip. I paid little attention to the few seals loafing in the shallows when I launched a nine-inch bone-colored Doc seaward. The lure soared in a long arc swaying back and forth before touching down and skipping off the top of a wave. A gorilla bluefish exploded from the foam and grabbed the lure mid-air taking it down in a beautifully violent strike. I heaved back, felt the rod surge, and heard the reel's drag surrender yards of line. I settled in for what should have been a long, delicious battle.

But something went wrong. Halfway in, the bluefish began jackknifing wildly on the surface. The ocean surged in a terrible heave, and something yanked the fish beneath the waves straight out of a scene from the movie *Jaws*. Moments later, a quarter-ton gray seal came up with the bluefish—*my* bluefish—squarely in its maw, the tail and head hanging limply on either side. I pulled back as hard as I could, hoping to free the fish. Prying a gazelle from a lion would have been easier. The seal then dove, dumping fifty yards of line as an afterthought. With no other choice, I snubbed down on the reel and broke off, losing the fish, leader, and my $20 lure.

Something else was lost, too. A spot I joyfully had fished every fall since 2005 was no longer mine. It now belonged to the seals. Some may see this as a sort of comeuppance—nature reclaiming what once was hers. But there was something unnatural about it, too, with the seals keying in on surfcasters' catches for their next meal.

And I don't blame the seals. They are doing what evolution has taught them: seek out the weak and injured. A hooked fish happens to match that perfectly. But maybe a released fish does, too. A friend recently spotted two dead bass in the thirty-pound class washed up on a beach with their tails gnawed off. Were they set free by anglers only to be taken by opportunistic grays? Not sure. What I do know for sure is the three filleted bass carcasses I found on another beach a few days later—fish in the twenty-five to forty-pound class and clearly over the size limit—were killed by selfish humans who know better.

Since the first seal incident, I have revisited the North Rip a few times and caught a handful of fish. But each cast I make is filled with trepidation. Growing numbers of cruising seals seem ever more emboldened. Hook a fish, and you need to crank it in as quickly as possible with the very real fear that a big horsehead is about to eat your lunch. On my last trip there, a friend let a bluefish take one run too many and wound up reeling in half a fish head. At least he got his lure back.

My experience on Block Island is far from isolated. I have read anglers' posts on various fishing message boards, and they are increasingly grim. Cape Cod's National Seashore, once the sacred haunt of legendary surfcasters like the late Tony Stetzko who beached a world-record seventy-three-pound striper there in 1981, is now devoid of anglers due to seals pouncing on virtually every hooked fish. Flyrodders are giving up on Nantucket's Great Rip and its false albacore for the same reason. A friend's annual group trip to Brewster Flats to sight cast for stripers, organized through a local fly shop, has been permanently canceled due to seals.

I have also read on message boards how to "fix" the seal problem. Some posts are nonsensical, testosterone-charged rants threatening to sneak into seal haul-out areas at night to shoot them. Besides the obvious illegality and danger, let's unpack that idea. Legal or not, any seal cull would most likely not work. The first issue is scale. There are perhaps one hundred thousand seals currently in New England waters. How many would need to be killed to "control" them? Hundreds? Thousands? Tens of thousands? And how would you do it? Round them up and blast away? Poison them? Club their babies? What do a hundred dead seals look like floating in the ocean?

Remember, most of the public adores seals. There are seal-watching cruises, annual seal counts, seal plush, and seal T-shirts. Imagine the public's response if a state or federal agency announced a seal cull. There would be global outrage, on par with the outcry from Japan's horrific Taiji dolphin drive chronicled in the 2010 Academy Award–winning documentary *The Cove*. And all of this carnage just to satisfy some anglers who want to fish for stripers? Sorry, but it is just not going to happen.

Others suggest a limited hunt for seals for their meat or skin. Here's the problem: there is no demand, and I doubt a startup that touts "sustainable seal products" would do well in today's market-place. This is not the Hudson's Bay Company circa 1830 selling seal jerky to go with your hardtack.

How about sharks to keep seals in check? Yes, great whites are visiting New England waters more frequently, and a few times each year beach-going tourists on Cape Cod are treated to a real-life Discovery Channel moment when a seal becomes shark food. But with low reproduction and a slow maturity rate, great white numbers would need sudden, orders-of-magnitude growth to make a dent in the seal population. And of course with more sharks around, the potential of injuries to swimmers increases. Witness the 2018 fatal shark attack of a surfer in Wellfleet.

So that leaves us anglers with one option: coexistence. The world is full of inconvenient wildlife. Elephants sometimes raid farmers' fields; tigers kill livestock; alligators eat poodles. Hell, bluefish eat stripers (and stripers eat bluefish). How we tolerate them is up to us. Do we play God and mow them all down, or accept and adapt to their presence? On Block Island, I have largely ceded my beloved North Rip to the marine mammals who were there first. Because to my mind, there is no other choice. And there are other places for me to cast.

PART VI
Chasing the Blitz

There's no waiting for friends during a blitz.
—WISELY ANONYMOUS FISHING FRIEND, 2022

THE DE-EVOLUTION
OF AN ANGLER

SURFCASTING FOR STRIPED BASS ONCE TOOK PLACE IN THE SHAD-ows. Striper anglers fished alone, and almost exclusively at night. If you drove along a lonely beach road at two o'clock in the morning, you might happen upon one of their rigs parked in a turnout, its telltale rod racks attached to the front bumper. This was not an invitation to join them for some casts, for they were universally tight-lipped and borderline mean. If you ran into one trudging back to their truck, an eleven-foot surf rod over one shoulder and a heavy canvas plug bag slung over the other, you prepared for surliness:

"Any luck?" you might bravely ask.

"Humph."

"Okay, have a good night!"

"Humph."

Damn, has that all changed.

I partially blame it on a single baitfish, the peanut bunker, the juvenile stage of the oily forage fish otherwise called menhaden or mossbunker. Call it one of the great mysteries of the ocean, but beginning in the early aughts—at least along many of the beaches I regularly fished—schools of peanuts began to consistently migrate in the fall. And they were audacious, showing up in broad daylight and often by the acre. Everything in the ocean seemed to want to eat them, from loons to humpback whales. Summer flounder, in hot pursuit, would fling themselves out of the water like skipping frisbees. Gangs of cormorants herded them into dense bait balls then snapped them up by the beakful. And yes, stripers couldn't resist peanuts either. The mysterious, moody, regal striped bass, the mercurial creature of darkness, suddenly got dumb.

Anglers quickly discovered daytime striper feeding frenzies, otherwise known as a "blitz," a term once reserved for when schools of hyper-aggressive bluefish would rip, tear, and shred their prey while churning the ocean into a saltwater latte. Striped bass now joined in on the fun, even muscling out the bluefish, now on the downward swing of a decades-long population cycle. Hordes of newly minted striper anglers began racking up catches in a single tide that previously may have taken entire seasons. Conversely, the nighttime fishery became increasingly spotty. It was as if the peanut bunker schools sucked stripers away from their midnight haunts into the midday sun. Day became night; night became day.

Striper anglers changed, too, becoming downright chatty about the whole thing. Perhaps it was generational, coupled with technology and social media, but many anglers posted and shared images and video of seemingly every fish they caught. If they hit a blitz, they texted their fishing friends to come join them. The surf turned into a sort of fishing rave with sometimes hundreds of anglers lining once-quiet beaches. The other big change was geographical. Over the last several years, my home waters of New Jersey, while always supporting a decent fall run, emerged as the premier spot for blitzing stripers, surpassing even storied Montauk. Look in parking lots along the more popular beaches like Sandy Hook or Island Beach State Park when the blitz is on, and you'll find license plates from the entire Eastern Seaboard. Yes, it's been that good.

Meanwhile, the old guard, misanthropes who wouldn't share spots with their own mothers, have largely vanished. A few still grumble about the days of yore when you could fish an entire tide with no one in sight. Many have gone on to the Big Wash where sixty-pounders storm a lively surf on moonless nights that never end—and with no one around to bother them. I'm sure they are happier there. Others, perhaps, are still out there, prowling somewhere in the darkness, but you would never know it.

Today I find myself a semi-reformed, once-secretive nighttime striper angler who now openly chases the daytime blitz. I have replaced my headlamp with sunscreen and binoculars. Fishing days are spent dashing from beach town to beach town glassing the water looking for telltale signs of wheeling gulls, breaking fish, or even just gatherings of anglers and fishing trucks. Often, I don't even leave the comfort of my home and instead study webcams strategically positioned up and down the coast searching for clues. Call it channel surfcasting.

There is lots of downtime between blitzes—sometimes days can pass between catches. Wader-clad anglers linger in parking areas exchanging intel: "It's dead now but I heard it was decent at first light." "Good up north yesterday." "Outgoing's been better than incoming." "My buddy beached a forty-pounder two days ago." Phone screens are shared showing off recent catches or videos of bass chasing bunker at your feet. I find myself an active participant in these conversations, fighting back repressed nighttime striper instincts to remain silent.

In the end, a blitz can be visually spectacular, even addicting in its own way. Sprinting down the beach while a school of big bass tears into bunker schools while hundreds of gulls screech overhead is one of the great thrills in angling. Yet I can't help but think something is lost when you crane in one fish just so you can cast out again and immediately hook another. It's like hitting the local White Castle for a sack of sliders. Yeah, it's satisfying, but it's not the superfood of a singular hard-earned fish. But as striper fishing continues to evolve into something I no longer recognize, I suspect I will find myself pulling up to the drive-thru window more and more and saying: "Sure, supersize me."

A NOVEMBER BLITZ

TODAY BEGINS WITH WHALES.

Just after sunrise, I park at a dead-end road lined with garish Jersey Shore beach mansions. I step out of my car for a quick look at surf conditions. Decent swell and some nice whitewater. No one is fishing, though, just a few trucks idling with the heat on, rods still clamped to roof racks. I chat with one guy, sipping coffee with his window down, who says he's been here a while. "Nothing happening. Just those whales," he says, pointing. Sure enough, two humpbacks spout about a half mile off the beach. We watch them slowly steam south. A jogger in a sweatsuit shows up. I try pointing out the whales to him, but he keeps saying: "I don't see them." Hard to miss a whale, so maybe he needs new glasses.

I decide to follow them, so I drive to a beach club maybe a half mile away. It's closed for the season, but its parking lot overlooks the ocean. The humpbacks are closer now, and I watch them with binoculars from a seawall. Then I see bunker splashing . . . then bass busting on them. The school moves in front of a jetty within casting range. Gulls whirl. Here we go.

In a flurry, I suit up and hurry toward the surf. The bass briefly erupt again, this time a hundred yards down the beach, but then they're gone just as quickly. Another surf fisherman shows up, and we fish side by side in the pocket alongside a jetty. He misses a blowup on a popper and I miss a thump on a bucktail, but that's it. So I leave, driving south through Asbury Park, once a sketchy ghost town, but now booming with hip, overpriced hotels. I stop at the next town south, Ocean Grove, known for its impeccably restored Victorian beach bungalows. I walk to the beach with my binoculars and see birds a half mile south in Bradley Beach, so I move again.

In Bradley, a few guys are casting and gulls circle, so I grab the rod and surf bag. Birds swing in close to a jetty, and I see bass busting. I pass a guy landing a schoolie on a swim shad in the pocket on the north side. Not wanting to crowd him, I set up on the south side and immediately get a swing and miss on a Spook, but then nothing. By now, the birds are a long cast away. So I put on a tin and boom it out. I miss a strike but then go fishless on my next half dozen casts. I switch to a big bucktail and red trailer and finally land a small fish—maybe four pounds. Meanwhile, the guy fishing the swim shad is putting on a clinic, landing schoolie after schoolie, and two guys now set up next to him are hooking up on pencils. Then Swim Shad Guy lands a thirty-four-incher (I hear him announce the length of the fish to the world). Now a fly-fisherman has since joined the party, clambering onto the jetty and landing two schoolies one after the other. Meanwhile, I'm cycling through my surf bag without a touch. Clearly, I'm in the wrong spot despite a pod of about fifty adult bunker swimming in figure 8s around my feet and looking terrified. So, I make the walk of shame and join the lineup. I see a fish swirl in the whitewater in tight, so on a hunch, I switch to a three-quarter-ounce lime-green bucktail and it works. I quickly land four schoolies while the rest of the guys go cold. So there. But then the bite dies altogether, and guys start wandering off the beach. I leave, too.

I drive back north and wind up at the beach club parking lot from this morning with the ocean view. Nothing happening, so I eat a quick lunch and brew a pot of coffee on my camp stove. A guy pulls up in a pickup with rod racks, and we begin chatting. I've come to learn that anglers looking for blitzes are far more talkative than usual tight-lipped striper guys. There's a lot of exchange of info: where you just came from, what you saw, and who caught what yesterday. I guess we're all playing the same lottery. Then he gets a call from one of his buddies that it's happening at a beach twenty miles south of us, and he leaves. I decide that's too far for me, so I opt to stay and finish my coffee. Birds begin circling maybe a quarter mile down the beach, so I get in my car and drive a few blocks. There's an older guy at the end of the street with binoculars. He's watching three anglers cast next to a jetty. He tells me they are picking at schoolies. I'm thinking about grabbing my gear to join them when they all start running south. I look beyond them. Birds in tight. I hop in my car to make another two-block move to intercept them.

When I get to the beach, twenty guys are already lined up with a few bent rods, and birds and bass blitz in front of them. I'm about to make my first cast, when the birds suddenly wheel north and begin diving along a jetty one hundred yards away. Anglers run past me to climb onto the rocks. But I notice there's no one fishing along the adjacent beach. On a hunch, I hurry past the scrum of anglers on the rocks, thinking the fish will move my way and I'll have them to myself—at least for a little while.

And it happens. A massive school of adult bunker and bass blows up right in front of me. I send a seven-inch Doc seaward. It lands in the melee, but there's so much bait I wind up snagging a bunker. The next cast touches down on the edge of the school and is immediately walloped. I set the hook and I'm in. A few minutes later, I slide a bulked-out twenty-pounder on the beach for a quick release. The main bunker school pushes past, but bass remain to pick off stragglers. They slash and boil everywhere—in the white water, in the breakers . . . everywhere. Several times I watch individual bunker make a sort of death spiral, then get inhaled in a giant slurp. A green wave curls, and I can clearly see a half dozen fifteen-pound stripers in tight formation just behind a hundred fleeing bunker.

Time either slows down or speeds up in a blitz. I'm honestly not sure how long the action goes on—maybe forty-five minutes, maybe an hour. What I do know is that the Doc and I can do no wrong. I land perhaps fifteen "overs"—fish over the legal limit of 31 inches—in nearly as many casts. By now, other anglers have joined me. The guy to my immediate right whoops with joy whenever his plug—or mine—gets crushed. Then a big bass slams my lure at the lip of a wave, thrashing wildly and really throwing water. It grinds out a long, low-gear run, and I lean back clutching the rod with both hands and enjoy the ride. Eventually I beach a thirty-pounder that looks like it's been wolfing down steroids instead of bunker.

The blitz ends, and I'm almost glad, as it starts to teeter on the precipice of gluttony—but not quite. I reel up my plug and walk up to the joyful angler who had been fishing next to me. He greets me with an enthusiastic "*Dude!*" and fist bumps me. We laugh and swap tales of our good fortune. Eventually, I wander back to my car in a sort of daze, covered in sweat and salt and sand and happy to be alive.

SOME FISHING
JOURNAL ENTRIES

NOVEMBER 18, 2024
If I talk to one more guy who tells me how great it was every other day I wasn't fishing this week, I am going to slit my wrists and bleed out on the beach. Most annoying was the older guy who said Sandy Hook was the best fishing he ever experienced on Thursday when I stayed home to do yardwork. When I told him that, he looked at me and with all sincerity said: "Man I'm really sorry." And when Rob and I were driving south on Tuesday to fish a beach deep into Ocean County, it turns out that if we only decided to stay and hit nearby North Beach on the Hook, we could have joined the two guys who said they had "thirty fish each up to forty pounds with no one around." Kill me.

NOVEMBER 22, 2024
Big bunker pushed over the bar in slow motion and formed this sort of enormous whirlpool, pushing a bow wave ahead of themselves. To see bass coming up in the middle of the school and willing to take your plug was beyond cool.

NOVEMBER 25, 2024
Turns out if I have fish breaking in front of me, I can go several hours without food, drink, or bathroom breaks.

A Blitz in Four Acts

Prologue

Bolstered—some may say frustrated—by recent reports, not to mention the live webcam footage showing epic fishing up and down Monmouth County, I decided that yesterday was the day for a November marathon. I packed the car with tackle, a cooler filled with the usual snacks and lunch, a jug of water, and my camp stove and coffee pot. I was out the door by 6:00 a.m. and would be home after dark. My strategy was simple: look for birds/cars/anglers. Minimize blind casting. Take breaks if nothing is happening. Check live fishing reports online. No commitments to any one spot unless I saw bent rods or breaking fish. Be prepared to move a lot. Be a gull.

Act I: Sunrise and Birds

My plan was to begin at Belmar, which is maybe twenty miles south of Sandy Hook and the site of the webcam blitz footage I found myself drooling over the day before. My GPS first took me through Bradley Beach, which is maybe a mile or so north. But when I made the turn south along the ocean at around 7:30 a.m., I immediately saw birds, so I parked and readied my gear alongside two other dudes who were doing the same. They hurried to the beach, and I was right behind them. It turned out to be largely a mirage, however, with gulls that at first looked close, but when you make your best cast you watch your lure land impotently 150 yards short. The gulls moved around quickly and zeroed in on only a few brief out-of-range blowups—not the carnage I saw on the webcams. Scattered boats and a few party boats moved around here and there. Dozens of surfcasters up and down the beach flailed away the entire time. A quarter mile away, I saw a rod bend and a single fish landed, but that was it. After an hour or so, it was time to move.

Act II: Tour of Monmouth County

I drove south through Belmar into Spring Lake, but the birds began to dissipate the farther I went. So, I made a U-turn and headed north again back through Belmar, Avon-by-the-Sea, and then Ocean Grove. Birds looked closer there, so I made some casts, but it was more of the same—fast-moving gulls and nothing close. Lots of anglers coming and going, and many tripped-out trucks with rod-racks driving back and forth. All of us looking for the same thing. After an hour, I headed north some more into Asbury Park and stopped at the boardwalk. There I had a nice chat with a serious surf guy a few years older than me with binoculars around his neck. It turns out we knew some of the same local sharpies who fished Sandy Hook back in the day. He was in on the blitz from the day before, fishing at West End, which is just south of Long Branch, and yeah, it was epic. "I had to crawl back to the car, I caught so many fish," he told me. Bastard. The whole time we watched birds briefly ball up then quickly break up. While we spoke, he took several calls and texts from buddies who were deployed at various other surf spots. But the reports were universal: nothing happening. So we parted ways wishing each other luck. I headed north some more through Loch Arbor and into opulent Deal with its crazy nouveau riche beach houses. I parked at a dead-end road with an ocean view. By now it was late morning, so I brewed some coffee on my camp stove, had some yogurt and a few dates, and watched some gulls maybe a half mile off the beach with a boat on them. After coffee, I trudged down to the surf and made some casts but raised nothing. I continued north.

Act III: A Taste of the Action

Now my plan was to hit West End where the crawling angler did so well, but I took a quick detour maybe a mile south heading to a public access in the town of Elberon. Lots of cars parked, so maybe some hope. I watched a guy in waders walk out of his car, look down the beach, then quickly walk back, grab his rod, and shuffle away. More hope. When I hit the sand, I saw two bent rods among a half dozen anglers, along with a few gulls maybe a hundred yards off the beach. I picked my spot, heaved out a seven-inch Doc, and walked it back. It made it maybe five yards before it cratered, and I set into a fat twelve-pounder—my first bass in two weeks and deeply satisfying. Then I hooked a smaller fish that looked maybe six pounds but shook off just before I beached it. A few other guys were hooking up around me. Most fish looked between ten and fifteen pounds. I had a few more blowups on the Doc and dropped a nicer fish that thrashed wildly but then shook off. But then a half hour passed with nothing else landed. Thinking the fish headed south, I headed back to the dead end with the ocean view but didn't see any birds. I decided it was time for a late lunch—canned tuna and bean salad that was quite delicious. But halfway through eating it, gulls began circling next to a jetty pocket. I grabbed my rod and surf bag and made my way to the surf, all while still eating tuna and bean salad with a fork—no easy feat. I made a cast with a Yo-Zuri Hydro Pencil. Halfway in, a bass took hard, and I landed a fat six-pounder. I thought I had stumbled into something, but it was not to be—just the one fish. But I did see a bald eagle flying among a few gulls; a flock of snow buntings, which I haven't seen in decades; and a pair of peregrine falcons oddly perched on some beach debris, probably eyeballing the buntings. It's not always about the fish.

Act IV: My Personal Blitz

It was getting late in the day, so I decided to head south one more time. The plan was to check out Loch Arbor, Asbury, Ocean

Grove, Bradley Beach, and Avon-by-the-Sea before winding up in Belmar where the original webcam blitz had taken place. Nothing doing until I hit Bradley, where I could see some birds over the dunes that looked close. I pulled over and scrambled onto the boardwalk for a quick look-see. There, just to the north, a handful of gulls picked at something in a jetty pocket. No one there, so I grabbed my rod and bag. As I approached, I could see the dark purple bruise of a school of peanuts. Then I saw a few blowups, and, praise the Fishing Gods, I had walked into a mini blitz with no other anglers around. It turned out they were not large fish—mostly schoolies between four and five pounds, though I eventually landed one that was around eight and had a nicer fish on that took line and sulked for a while before it shook off. And they were fussy for sure; many times, I cast into breaking fish with nothing to show for it. But enough missed swipes and blowups that every cast felt hopeful. It went on like that until nearly dark. And it was glorious: a lively surf, churned by a freshening southeast breeze with bass chasing peanuts into the breakers sometimes only a few yards away. All told, I landed four or five on a mix of Spooks, a Danny, and a one-ounce bucktail. Near the end of the session another angler joined me: a kid about fifteen years old who powered up on an e-bike and wore white rubber boots. He was a local sharpie, it turned out. He glanced at my tackle and asked how I liked my Van Staal and wanted to know what kind of St. Croix rod I was fishing. A budding tackle junkie. When he landed a four-pound fish, he asked me if they were all this small. I was incredulous, so I asked him: "What's your biggest fish?"

And perhaps hoping I would ask that very question, he quickly answered: "Fifty-one inches," and proceeded to show me a picture on his phone of him holding a fifty-pounder from the previous year, the little shit. Actually, he was a nice kid, and he wished me good luck, before zipping off for home on his e-bike just as the action died at dark.

MAX AND ME

MY COWORKER MAX ASKED ME TO TAKE HIM SURF FISHING, SO we agreed to meet on Sandy Hook one November morning. Max is originally from Pittsburgh and mostly a smallmouth and walleye guy. He never caught a striper before but told me he landed a few fluke a couple of years ago off a jetty while vacationing in Connecticut. So limited saltwater experience.

We met on the Hook a little after 5:00 a.m. and began casting along a rocky cove. A cold wind blew, and there was a strong north-south sweep, making it hard to stay in contact with your plug. By the time it got a little lighter, I had switched to a Hydro Pencil and, out of sheer will, coaxed a slightly-larger-than-rat-sized bass to grab it near some submerged boulders. I called Max over, positioned him in the spot, and told him where to cast. Then I backed off. Maybe twenty minutes later, I saw his rod bend and watched him beach a sixteen-incher—his first-ever striper. Pictures were taken and fists bumped.

By the time the sun came up, the action died. I could have called victory at this point and headed home, but we decided instead to grab breakfast then continue fishing somewhere else. We hit a diner in nearby Sea Bright. There, over eggs and coffee, we overheard some older, saltier guys sitting at the next table talking loudly about bunker and blitzing bass. I casually asked them where they were seeing fish. One of them said to me: "Everywhere!"

So I asked him again: "Yeah, but where??"

And he said: "You know, *everywhere!*"

We decided to see if *everywhere* meant the local beach behind the diner, so we walked there after breakfast. Conditions still looked sporty with the north wind not quitting and a lone center console getting tossed around among some birds working maybe a half mile off the beach. We decided to give it a try anyway but wound up with zilch. On the way back to our cars, we spoke with a few surfcasters standing around in the parking lot with idle rods. One of them told me about lots of fish at first light just to the north of where Max and I had fished earlier, and another guy in the group had them to the south. So, you know, everywhere.

We drove back to the Hook, where I decided to play a wild card and hit a spot on the bayside where I can sometimes eke out a bass on the outgoing. But after a long hike and an hour of fruitless casting, we headed back to our cars with nothing to show for it. By now it was high noon with a bright sun shining down—not the best conditions. But the wind had dropped off, so we decided to hit one last oceanside spot. We drove to the end of a beach road that looked out over the surf. All was quiet.

We easily could have quit at this point, but then Max said: "Hey, let's give a shot for a little while."

Sure, why not?

We walked north to a series of sandbars. Small rollers broke over them. We waded through a waist-deep trough, then stood knee deep on a bar and began casting poppers. It looked nice out there, but with no signs of bait or anything else, I figured I'd put in a half hour or so just to be a good host before we finally hung up our rods for the day.

About fifteen minutes in, a decent-sized bass crashed my Polaris, batting it out of the water but missing. Then maybe five casts later another good-sized fish swirled behind it but didn't commit. After that it went quiet for a while, and I cursed myself for not getting those bass to eat, as I was pretty sure that would be the last chance for the rest of the day. A few minutes later, a school of peanut bunker appeared just beyond the breakers—appearing like a thirty-foot-long dark amoeba with flashes of silver just beneath the surface. I told Max he should cast to the edge of the school, that maybe some bass were following them. He did, and I did, too, but nothing happened, and it started to look like a predator-free school of so-called happy bunker.

But then there was a blowup in the school, followed by another, and another. I had since switched to the Hydro Pencil but enticed nothing for the first few casts. I rifled through my plug bag and settled on a yellow Danny. It V-waked for a few feet before a bass grabbed it throwing water. After a short fight, I landed the fish—maybe a six-pounder. Now stripers could be seen crashing bunker schools up and down the beach. A full-blown blitz was developing.

Meanwhile Max foul-hooked a peanut bunker on his popper and told me he was going to sling it into the school thinking that a bass would eat it. I told Max, no, shake the bunker off the plug, and make a real cast. On cue, a pod of about a dozen bass erupted forty feet in front of him. I pointed and yelled: "*Cast! There! Now!*" He did and immediately hooked into a good striper. "*Nice!*" I yelled. Earlier, Max said he wanted to keep a bass for dinner, and since this fish looked legal sized, he began backing off the sandbar into the trough to eventually slide it onto the beach.

By now, a *National Geographic*–level spectacle was unfolding, with bass chasing bunker in the curl of the breakers, blowing up in the whitewater, and jetting past me in two feet of water. By the time I landed my third fish—an eight-pounder—I turned back to see how Max was faring. But instead of triumphantly beaching his first keeper striper, he seemed to be floundering in the trough. He still battled his fish, so I did what any good angler would do: I fired out another cast and hooked a bass—now about a ten-pounder. I looked back again and now saw Max crawling onto the beach somehow still holding his bent rod. Three beachgoers converged and seemed to be assisting him. He told me later that, when he backed into the trough, he stumbled and water immediately filled his waders since he had no wading belt. So by the time he made it to shore, he literally couldn't walk so he needed to belly up the beach like a seal. Fortunately, the beach walkers helped him; one of them took the rod and dragged the fish ashore—a keeper of about twelve pounds. Later, when I told my wife this story, she was shocked I didn't stop fishing and rush over to assist. Here's my take: when I saw Max still fighting the fish, I figured all was okay. Later, a straw poll among a few fishing friends revealed that—to a person—all would have done the same thing. My long-time fishing partner Jim even wrote: "As long as he wasn't yelling for help, or was on fire, you keep fishing. BLITZ!" Oh, and did I happen to mention I had just landed my sixth fish, about a fourteen-pounder? Max eventually emptied out his waders and triumphantly walked back to his car with his fish. I, on the other hand, fired out another cast and hooked another striper.

This blitz-of-the-ages continued, and the bass sizes steadily increased to the low teens, then mid-teens. And so it went for the next ninety minutes or so: a fish or at least multiple blowups on virtually every cast until the action began to slow. When I made my fifth fishless cast, I decided enough was enough and headed down the beach to my car, sometimes walking past more mini blitzes. But I was done. All told I probably released twenty stripers—maybe more. I truly lost count. The best one weighed seventeen pounds on my Boga Grip, but several were in that same range. As for Max, he had long since headed home, dripping wet but psyched he had a keeper in the cooler. He apparently texted me he was leaving, but I didn't hear it over the mayhem . . .

THE KID'S FIRST STRIPER

BEGINNING JUST AFTER COVID, I HAVE BEEN MENTORING A
local kid about the ways of the angle. He came to me by way of a
friend—he was the son of one of his coworkers. All the kid apparently wanted to do was fish, and his non-fishing parents remained
flummoxed. Could I please help? Why yes, yes I could.

I met the kid for the first time one afternoon at a local
park where I gave him some rudimentary fly-casting lessons
and advised him about some tackle purchases. Since then, we've
caught smallmouth, panfish, trout, and shad together, and I've
found him to be an attentive and patient angler.

Recently, the kid, now in college, said he wanted to try his
luck surfcasting for stripers. So I took him out the day after
Thanksgiving, and we had a biblical skunking, driving around the
North Jersey coast, hitting various access points, and seeing and
catching zilch. It happens. All too often.

A couple of weeks later, after he got home for winter break,
he wanted to give it another shot. On the day he could join me, I
had a feeling things might be slow due to the onset of southerly
winds, which always seem to shut down the fishing. But we went
anyway since there have been plenty of times this season that I
stayed home when conditions looked crappy, only to find out later
it went off.

We arrived around noon at a spot where I found some fast-moving schools earlier in the week on the same tide. But it was dead. As in dead-dead. Just the usual beach buggies meandering around and a handful of anglers wandering the beach like zombies in waders. A few gulls flew without purpose, and loons casually bobbed and dove in a rolling surf. We made some casts anyway, and the kid showed off a wooden metal-lipped swimmer he bought at a local tackle shop that had a nice V-waking action. We even saw a few beached peanut bunker flipping around in the rack-line that gave us hope. But there was nothing on them, it turned out, which surprised me.

We continued moving around to various beach lookouts, eventually stopping at one with a bench at the top of some dunes. There was a woman there staring at the waves looking concerned. She explained that she saw a man dive into the surf but could no longer see him. But then he bobbed up and began leisurely backstroking in the low fifty-degree water like it was the Fourth of July. She left, relieved. Then two surfcasters walked up scanning the otherwise empty ocean. I pointed out the polar-bear swimmer, and one guy—a local, I guess—told me he is out there every day. The other guy went on about the benefits of cold-water swimming as he smoked a joint. The swimmer eventually came ashore, dried himself off, walked past us and drove off in a beat-up sedan that needed a muffler. I would have thought someone who does cold-water swimming every day would be more into car maintenance, but that's me.

So if all of this sounds like filler for an otherwise fishless afternoon—it is. But then I had an idea: during a recent blitz, I fished next to a local sharpie for a while, and we chatted when the action ended. His name was Mark, and we agreed to swap numbers and keep each other informed if we see any action. And we have: I texted him brief dispatches from some recent trips, which he appreciated. In my phone he comes up as Striper Guy Mark. Yesterday morning, he sent me a report of decent fishing the night before at a bayside spot I had never fished before. So, I decided to text him looking for more info. He sent me a pin, the tide he fished, lures he used, and even agreed to meet me there at seven o'clock. Jackpot.

So, the kid and I stayed where we were and fished until dark (dead-dead-dead), then took a long break at a local diner to wait for the tide to turn. We parked where Striper Guy Mark instructed, then followed a trail that ended at a point extending into the bay. When we began casting, the tide had just started its ebb. Then I heard a sound that gave me joy, like hearing the voice of a departed friend from long ago: a striper popping out there in the darkness, then another and another. It was the sound I used to hear on the bayside of Sandy Hook for so many enjoyable seasons that has since gone quiet for unknown reasons.

Most of the pops sounded out of range, but a few were closer. As we cast, I was quickly reminded that popping stripers are no pushovers, particularly when it's glass calm. A half hour went past with nothing to show for it. Eventually, though, my plug stopped, then churned, and I eventually beached about a four-pound striper. This astounded the kid who had never seen one before and couldn't believe how huge it looked. This brought me back to my very first party boat trip circa 1981 when someone boated a six-pound bluefish that to my young eyes looked like it weighed at least sixty.

Unfortunately, my lone striper was it for the night's action. The popping slowed to maybe one every few minutes, and even Striper Guy Mark, who had since showed up, couldn't get a strike. The kid and I eventually left. Mark stayed, texting me that he wound up with two bass plus a missed hit.

A week later, I convinced the kid to give it one more shot for stripers. I picked him up the next day at 6:00 a.m. Our record so far was 0–2, but I still felt hopeful. The day before, on various Ocean County webcams, even though the surf looked blown out in the westerly gale, I could still see clouds of gulls beyond the breakers and even a few whales spouting. So clearly lots of bait still lingered. And the wind was predicted to lay down overnight, so I imagined a clear, calm, hopefully fish-filled surf. The kid was excited on the drive down, and he even asked if we could stop at a tackle shop on the way home so he could buy a surfcasting outfit with some advance Christmas money he scored (he had been borrowing one of my extra outfits).

But when we got to the beach, it was, in fact, dead. And freaking cold. A biting west wind blew down the beach, and the surf still ran big and slightly stained. We could see a sparse lineup of surfcasters and beach buggies, but no clusters of activity. Gulls once again appeared scattered except for the ubiquitous cloud two miles off the beach. We did see one short landed, which briefly gave us hope, but the long-drawn-out photo shoot of the poor fish that followed, plus the lack of other action among anyone else, did not inspire confidence. So we moved around, which frankly had been getting old this late in the season.

Eventually, we picked a spot, rigged up, and cast a while. We even saw another small bass landed and spoke with two other anglers who each beached one earlier. So, a slow pick at best. I could tell the kid's enthusiasm was rapidly ebbing with the tide. And I didn't blame him. At one point, he said he needed to catch at least something, like when he fishes for trout or smallmouth. I countered as best I could, telling him things like: "Yeah, but when it happens in the surf, it's *amazing*." I was sounding like the Atlantic salmon anglers I met on the Margaree River in the mid-2000s, who assured me how great it would be when I eventually hooked a big salmon on a dry fly, which never happened. And that's why I'm not an Atlantic salmon fisherman. Then to make things worse, between beach changes the kid said he no longer wanted to hit the tackle shop on the way back, so I was rapidly losing this once eager striper ward.

By late morning with not even a tap, it was clear this was not our day, so I asked if he wanted to head home and he said yes.

So, game pretty much over. But then I asked him if he wanted to drive straight home or perhaps mosey up the coast, just in case we saw something happening along the way. He chose the latter, so maybe there was still a glimmer of hope.

We began the usual northward coastal trek, past Manasquan, Sea Girt, and Spring Lake. Along the way we saw lots of surfers taking advantage of the large rolling breakers, but virtually no surfcasters and no birds.

When we reached Belmar, I saw a few gulls working close to shore. I pulled over. We got out of the car and watched them from the boardwalk. Maybe a dozen gulls hovered over knee-deep water breaking on a sandbar. I studied them with binoculars hoping to see a bust or a swirl beneath them but saw nothing. But then a gull dipped and came up with a silvery sand eel. Then a second bird did the same. I theorized out loud that sand eels were getting swept over the sandbar into a deeper trough that ran against the beach. I told the kid the spot looked interesting. Even though it was now high noon with a bright sun and the tide about to die, we should make some final casts. It was a Hail Mary, bottom of the ninth, two outs, two strikes, halfcourt-shot-at-the-buzzer, and all that.

We geared up one last time and made a final slog to the beach. I gave the kid a half ounce rubber sand eel jig and told him to cast into the trough. Then I gave him room, heading down the beach one hundred yards. Gulls continued to catch sand eels even though I couldn't see them in the stained water. I was working a small bucktail when I noticed the kid slowly backing toward the beach. Could it be? Then I saw the bent rod. Is it possible? Then, the ocean parted and, unbelievably, amazingly, and gloriously, the Fishing Gods presented him with his first-ever schoolie, a perfect four-pounder. The kid, obviously jazzed, took a gigabyte worth of images and video, and I didn't blame him. Then he released the bass, our only fish of the day, and properly celebrated by stopping at a tackle shop and picking up a shiny new surf outfit . . .

SWEEPS WEEK

RECENTLY I BEGAN REFERRING TO MY MULTI–BEACH TOWN blitz-hunts as "sweeps." They take place along the two oceanfront counties in New Jersey where one is likely to find a blitz: Monmouth, along the northern coast, and Ocean just to its south. Ergo, there can be Monmouth County Sweeps or Ocean County Sweeps, or if I'm feeling particularly ambitious (or desperate), a Multi-County New Jersey Sweep (MCNJS), which includes both counties. With that geographical orientation out of the way, here's how the last week in November 2024 went down.

I met Rob Maass for a marathon MCNJS on Tuesday. We rendezvoused at the Jon Bon Jovi rest stop (yes, that's really what it's called) at 5:45 a.m. Rob made great time driving from Brooklyn noting how uncongested New York roads are at 4:30 in the morning. We decided to take separate cars, so Rob followed me southward deep into Ocean County to the town of Lavalette.

There, Striper Guy Mark scored big time last Saturday with bass into the forties (pounds, not inches). He texted me images the following day and they were jaw-dropping—bunker-stuffed fish as thick as your torso. But alas, it was not happening for Rob and me on this windy morning. We watched the usual beach buggies scattered around along with a decent amount of surfcasters. But as we glassed the scene, we saw no bent rods and noted that, while there were plenty of gulls flying around, none worked over any sort of bait. So, we bounced around, venturing as far south as Seaside Park before turning back north. No birds, no fish. Nothing.

We stopped at the stylish beach town of Bayhead where we ran into another angler with binoculars. He confirmed Saturday's mayhem, gushing about catching unlimited thirty-pounders blah, blah, blah. Meanwhile, gulls picked in the shallows, enough that Rob and I geared up and made some casts. But it turned out to be fool's gold, so we left after a half hour.

We continued our northward sweep, crossing the Manasquan River and entering southern Monmouth County. Then came a dispatch from Striper Guy Mark who often monitors beach cams from home. "GO TO DEAL," he texted, "SEEING FISH ON TOP." We hurried to an access along a dead-end road among Deal's ubiquitous beachfront palaces. But by the time we parked and walked to the beach, the surf looked quiet. Our marathon began to feel like a slog.

We returned to our cars and pushed north into the town of Long Branch. Rob followed as I made a lazy turn onto a beach road. By now, I expected nothing. But as often happens in blitz fishing, nothing became everything. In front of us, thousands of gulls hovered just off the beach while hundreds of anglers fired casts into the surf. Meanwhile, fishing trucks were lurching into the few remaining parking spots along the ocean as decked-out surf anglers jogged down the boardwalk toward the action. It. Was. On.

Rob got lucky and parked right away. I pulled down a side street. No visible spots at first, but then lights blinked on an SUV. Someone was leaving. I pulled behind it and anxiously waited. Two well-dressed older women slowly got in, adjusted the mirrors, checked their cell phones, got back out for some reason then got back in, and then checked their cell phones one last time before slowly driving off. A year of my life had just passed, but I managed to screech into the spot, grab my tackle, and sprint to the beach, catching up with Rob.

We chose a gap in the crowd and waded to a submerged sandbar adjacent to a jetty. The wind had dropped off, but occasional chest-high rollers broke, and we had to leap over them. Two guys on either side of us fought and eventually landed bass in the twenty-pound range. But for whatever reason, Rob and I couldn't score despite bombarding the surf in front of us. Down the beach maybe one hundred yards away, a woman fought a fish for several minutes, slowly walking it back to shore. When she beached it, it looked seriously big. Later when I walked past her, she told me it weighed between forty and forty-five pounds. She went on to tell me about the larger one she had released earlier, and then showed me the broken handle of her reel. She said she was heading back home to get a backup. Badass.

The action slowed when we noticed anglers hustling north. Rob and I joined, stopping at a jetty where a few bass chased bunker a short cast away. A waderless angler with a dog at his side stood high on the beach casting. He cheerfully asked us if we caught any yet. We told him no, and he went on to tell us it had been going off for the last two hours and that he landed twenty fish already. This sounded like an invitation, so I asked if we could join him since it was a tight spot and there were other anglers just to our right. He said: "Sure; I live just up the road so I can fish whenever I want." *What a nice, pleasant fellow*, I thought.

I just made a cast when the spiteful Fishing Gods decided, for reasons known only to them, that right now would be a good time to unleash a forty-yard braid tangle on my reel (don't tell them I said this, but the Fishing Gods can be real assholes). With bass chasing bunker in front of me, I had to peel off tangled braid, cut it, and retie. While this was going on, I heard not-so-friendly words exchanged between Rob and the waderless guy who apparently kept casting over Rob's line. Turns out, this pleasant fellow was kind of a dick. And worse, a bad caster.

After I restrung my rod and retied the leader, we decided to head to the other side of the jetty. There we spotted a living room–sized school of busting stripers heading our way. Seconds later they came up massively and directly in front of us. I fired out another cast and, God no, got my second forty-yard tangle. What did I do to provoke the Fishing Gods to strike down upon me with such great vengeance and furious anger? With my reel literally cocooned in braid, I had to just stand there and take it, watching dozens of bass maraud bunker literally at my feet. Rob, unfettered, pitched his bucktail into the melee and instantly hooked up. I watched him fight and eventually land a twelve-pounder. After the release, Rob's line somehow got tangled in my mess, so I had to cut off his leader and hand it back to him. Rob retied and cast. Bass continued to boil. I continued to boil. I knew there was a fully rigged extra rod back at my car—now maybe three-quarters of a mile away. It became painfully obvious that I needed to get the hell out of there and go get it. I took a deep breath, then hauled ass, setting some sort of land-speed record for a middle-aged guy in waders while swearing. Along the way, I called Mark and let him know that it was on. He thanked me and said he might see me later. By the time I swapped out my rod and joined Rob back on the beach, the action had slowed as I knew it would. While I was gone, he landed three more—two fish at thirty inches each and one a little larger.

We made our way back to our cars. Along the way, occasional fish still broke water, and anglers beached a few more. But overall, the action waned. We loaded our gear and drove north to the next beach access. There, we found more birds and dozens of anglers lined up, but they only picked at bass here and there. Offshore, maybe a quarter mile out, we watched enormous blowups from what looked like monster-sized stripers, but they never came within casting range.

By now, it was almost three o'clock in the afternoon. We had been fishing on and off for nearly eight hours. I suggested to Rob we continue north. First we stopped at Monmouth Beach. Nothing happening. Next was Sea Bright. Dead. Then Rob announced he had reached the finish line of his marathon, and I understood. He broke down his gear and drove off to Brooklyn. To wrap up my sweep, I decided to make one last stop at Sandy Hook. But it turned out the Hook, too, was quiet. Just as I began peeling off my sweaty, disgusting waders, my phone rang. It was Striper Guy Mark. "Where are you, brother?" he said. "There's fish all over here in Long Branch." I made a U-turn and sped back south, determined. In case one needed reminding, I had not caught jack or shit all day. And jack left town.

By the time I made the turn along the Long Branch boardwalk, it looked like a shopping mall on Black Friday. Trucks and fishing cars had crammed into every parking space. After some frantic searching, I found a spot a half mile from the action then hurried down the beach toward a Woodstock-sized crowd of surfcasters. When I reached the first outer bands of anglers, I watched a guy make a long cast, then hook, fight, and release a twenty-pounder. As I passed him, a school of bass erupted one hundred feet away. Mayhem ensued. Anglers jammed next to each other, shoulder to shoulder, firing out casts. Then every other rod bent with stripers. I stood behind them, waiting for a gap where I could squeeze in. Two anglers tangled, forcing them off the line, so I jumped into the breach and got off a cast with a stubby pencil. The lure arced, then touched down into the center of the blast zone. I cranked twice then watched a bass cream the plug. A few minutes later, I beached a ten-pounder. Finally—my long-suffering itch was scratched. By the time I released the fish, the school had moved on, so I continued down the beach until I found Striper Guy Mark heaving a surface plug stratospherically far.

We hadn't seen each other since last season, so we hugged like reunited brothers. He introduced me to his crew of three other serious-looking anglers, all of whom were less than half my age. They all fist-bumped me, which made me feel cool for a minute or two. Then we exchanged info. Mark released a forty-six-incher an hour ago and had a smaller, legal fish on the beach for his wife. His friends released a few as well. While we spoke, anglers around us still picked away at bass, mostly by casting small rubber shads. We joined them as the sun lowered behind us, but the action quickly tapered off. When the sun dipped below the horizon, I could still see a few fish blitzing well off the beach. A few minutes later it ended, and a skyline of beach condos and high rises twinkled behind us. More fist bumps to Mark and his crew before parting ways. I walked in the door at 6:30. Just one fish during this MCNJS, but of course, it was worth it.

A few days later, I met Rob along with John Waldman for an Ocean County Sweep (OCS) beginning again in Lavalette. Rob made it to the beach first, texting an image of an eight-pound bass he released on his third cast on a spoon. Then I showed up and, a few casts in, had a swing and a miss on a Doc, while Rob missed a couple of blowups on a Polaris. Twenty minutes later, John arrived after fighting some Long Island traffic. We began to see a few bunker schools making their way down the beach, with stripers occasionally busting on them. A few surf anglers around us landed fish, but the school moved past quickly. I decided to check in by text with my virtual wingman, Striper Guy Mark. He directed me southward to Island Beach State Park. Once again, he had been monitoring webcams from home and saw gulls diving and a crowd of anglers casting. But he suggested I stop along the way at Seaside Park where he also spotted birds and anglers. Since I have learned not to make a move without Striper Guy Mark's counsel, we caravaned to a beach access at Seaside. There, we watched a few surfcasters each land a single bass casting diamond jigs, but not enough action to tempt us into joining them.

Instead, I glassed the water with binoculars, slowly scanning farther and farther south, until. . . . Oh. My. God. Two miles away, it looked like the Dunkirk evacuation with dozens of boats hovering just off the beach and a thick black blob of anglers stretching literally to the horizon. Um, let's fish there. Now. Our caravan continued south. We stopped at the first parking lot and spoke with an angler who told us he had been catching bass literally all morning at an access we had just passed. He claimed they were still hitting and started scrolling his phone to show us images of the action. After a couple of pictures of nice stripers, I told him: "Those are great fish, but we have to go now." He laughed and understood. U-turns were made, and we hastily parked along the side of the road joining dozens of other cars and trucks.

We followed a beach trail that wound through bayberry and beach plum and eventually gave way to dunes. Beyond that I could hear the surf and the cries of gulls. My pace quickened. We emerged onto an open beach with fifty anglers lined up and perhaps twenty bent rods. Holy crap, the guy wasn't lying. I stepped up, made a cast, and had a missed crash on my Doc. I looked over just as Rob hooked a ten-pounder that he eventually released. But then it went quiet, and I feared we once again walked into the tail end of the action.

A few minutes later, another school of bunker swept past with bass giving chase. Anglers cast and hooked a few fish. And it continued on and off for much of the afternoon. Waves of bunker would move down the beach and into the breakers. Pods of bass periodically blew up on them, sometimes in true blitz mode, other times singles or pairs would careen out of the water in burst of silvery peanuts. But with so many dense schools of bunker around, the bass proved to be fussy. It reminded me of fly fishing for trout during a blizzard caddis hatch—too much of the real thing to regularly fool a fish.

The visuals, nevertheless, were stunning. Bunker schools sometimes so thick, waves seemed to gelatinize into more fish than water. Stripers body-surfed in the curls of breakers, a confetti of fleeing bunker spraying just ahead of them. An undulating bunker mass darkened the shallows with bass exploding on them leaving behind blossoms of sand-colored bottom. A rod length away, a fifteen-pound bass casually swam past in knee-deep water, parting bunker like Moses and the Red Sea.

Still, if I kept casting, a bass would eventually find my plug. I wound up landing six on a very expensive, wooden stubby pencil that must be carved by Trappist monks based on the outrageous price I paid at a local tackle shop. I walked onto the beach disliking it, because it had so far barely produced, but walked off coddling it as a favorite. John had a solid fish grab a Kastmaster at the lip of a breaking wave and eventually beached what he said was a ten-pounder, but I say it went to eleven. Rob scored on a Kastmaster, too.

Late in the day, Rob, John, and I sat on the sand, tired and basking in the afternoon sun. We watched a ball of gulls down the beach a quarter mile away and debated whether they worked over bass or just bait. We had already been fooled earlier in the day, so there was room for discussion. Suddenly heads and tails ripped the surface. Debate over. We chased the school down, and I managed a long cast. A half turn of the reel and I was in. A few minutes later, I beached a thick eight-pounder. Rob scored, too, with a similar-sized fish. John worked the whitewater on the far side of the bar, but the fish had already moved off, continuing their southward migration to the Chesapeake. With the sun setting over Barnegat Bay, we decided to call it a session.

We officially ended the sweep in a booth at one of New Jersey's ubiquitous diners, swapping stories over coffee, cheeseburgers, and homemade soup. That night, I received a report from Striper Guy Mark who scored with teen-sized fish on plugs and teasers after dark at an undisclosed location.

WE ARE GULLS

We loaf until bait sprays and bass boil
Then we swarm and squawk and argue and fight
We chase down the lucky among us who has landed the single fish
When the blitz ends, we gather and gossip waiting for more
—SS

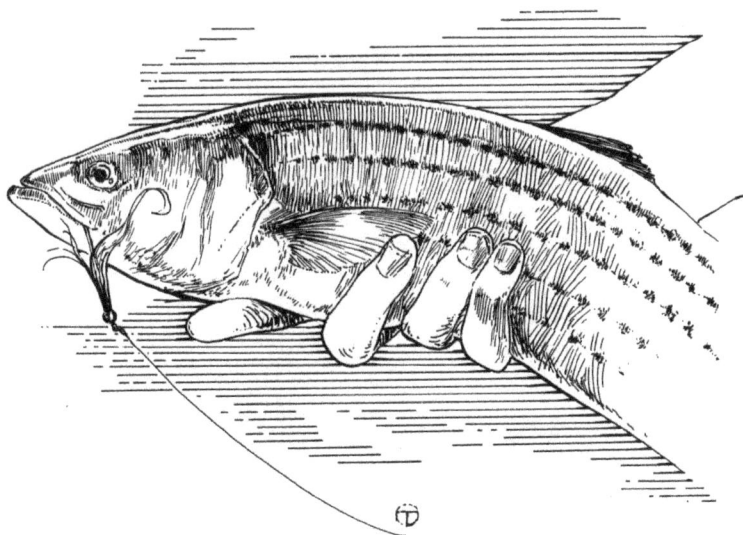

PART VII

WITH ROD TUBE IN HAND

At least he's not in some tavern!

—MY GRANDMOTHER, 1989

A Port of Call
Snags an Angler

Only a fool would cast a fishing lure from the ninth-floor balcony of an anchored 923-foot cruise ship tied up to the dock at Bermuda's Kings Warf. But when a pack of voracious jacks explodes under a school of bait, even if it is seventy vertical feet to the water, the temptation can be too much.

Giant cruise ships do not cater to anglers. That is, unless you want to spend up to $1,000 for a prearranged shore excursion with a local charter boat. On cruises, gambling, drinking, and of course, overeating remain the encouraged activities. Trolling and jigging are not. All of this leaves the do-it-yourself fisherman—the guy who happens to slip a rod tube and a box of lures or flies into his suitcase—feeling a little desperate.

This is why I found myself casting on deck 9, yet not fully thinking through what might happen if I actually hooked something. Would a thrashing jack need to be hauled in hand over hand, past the disco on deck 7 and the honeymooning couple on deck 8?

As it turned out, the question was academic. Despite my best casts, I only briefly hooked a single fish, and it managed to shake the lure free just before I clumsily attempted to crane it skyward.

The next day I walk off the gangplank armed with a bus schedule and a tourist map in search of a spot somewhere along Bermuda's varied shoreline where I could fish. I had visited one of the island's more famous bathing beaches the day before. But I found it contained a Jersey Shore–sized crowd, with most of them, it seemed, originating from my own cruise ship. An errant cast here might result in a hooked thong or Speedo. Or worse.

A dot on the map showed a tiny municipal park and protected beach that seemed as if it might be away from the cruise ship crowd. I took a gamble and got off at the closest bus stop and found myself all alone—an encouraging sign. A short walk down a quiet residential street ended at a small, pretty park with palm trees and a group of children noisily splashing in shallow water. Beyond them, a several-acre flat covered with turtle grass swayed with the tide.

A shape in the water swam toward me seemingly oblivious to the commotion. I strained to look. Bonefish. It swam closer. A big bonefish—eight pounds, easy. I glanced around looking for the inevitable flats boat or at least some other wading anglers. There were none. Bonefishing may be high religion in places like the Florida Keys and the Bahamas, but apparently in Bermuda, with its distracting rum swizzles and pink sand, they go largely ignored.

Not by me. The contents of my rod tube and backpack were disgorged on a towel and an eight-weight fly rod quickly assembled. A minute later, I found myself casting to perhaps the world's greatest shallow-water gamefish as a six-year-old girl bobbed a few yards away in water wings.

But each of my casts went ignored. Every few minutes, another bonefish would ghost down the beach, only to turn up its pointy snout at virtually anything I put in front of it. Twice a fish turned and tracked the fly for a yard, leaving me weak kneed before it vanished in the turtle grass. This behavior confirmed what scant information I had already gleaned about Bermuda's bonefish: they rank among the most selective in the world.

Eventually, I, too, became distracted, particularly when several two-to-three-foot barracuda appeared along the beach with the flooding tide. A well-placed wooden popper cast with a spinning rod might be more fun than vainly casting flies to bonefish with PhDs. This, coupled with the fact that my cruise ship departed for New York in less than two hours, made my decision an easy one.

So I stowed the fly rod and began firing long casts along the tidal flat, briskly retrieving the popper like a fleeing needlefish. One of the barracuda could not resist. It streaked across the surface and crashed the lure, hooking itself then dumping fifty feet of line from my reel. Its next run began with a greyhound leap and ended with violent head shakes resonating to the cork of my light spinning rod.

By now, some of the local youngsters had gathered, and they squealed when I eventually slid a silvery five-pound barracuda onto the beach. The popper hung on the outside of its jaw, thankfully away from its sinister-looking teeth. I held the fish for the youngsters to admire, and the brave ones touched it just before I let it go back into the shallows.

I continued to fish for another half hour, raising a half dozen more barracuda, solidly hooking two but losing them both. A three-foot houndfish, a bizarre serpentlike fish with a long bony snout joined in, grabbing the lure and jumping a dozen times before it, too, threw the hook.

Then it was time to leave before my ship sailed. I broke down both rods then walked to the waiting bus. I took a short, satisfying ride, soaked from the waist down and with pinkish sand still between my toes. In another hour, we would begin the 750-mile cruise back to New York. No trolling allowed.

FISHING IN THE PANAMA
CANAL IS KIND OF WEIRD

SOMETIMES WE FIND OURSELVES IN STRANGE PLACES WITHOUT
a fly rod.

Like in the Panama Canal. Surrounded by tarpon.

It was a work trip and an important one. The nineteenth con-
ference of the parties of the Convention on International Trade
in Endangered Species (CITES CoP19) had gathered in Panama
to decide the fate of hundreds of wildlife species threatened by
trade—everything from African elephants to tiny glass frogs.

By the end of week 1, CITES delegates passed major new
protections to safeguard dwindling populations of hammerheads
and other sharks—the first of what would become a string of
victories announced during the CoP. So, during the weekend
break between negotiations, a few of us decided to make some
celebratory casts. We asked around and found a tour operator who
arranged a half day trip to fish for tarpon in the former Panama
Canal Zone. How we'd fish for them, we weren't sure since none
of us brought our own tackle.

The Panama Canal's tarpon are, as my favorite philosopher
Bob Ross might say, a happy accident. They ascended through
locks from the Atlantic in the mid-1920s and prospered in Lake

Gatun, the twenty-one-mile-long impoundment that oceangoing vessels must navigate between oceans. (Some tarpon passed all the way through to the Pacific, establishing a feral population as far south as the Colombia/Ecuador border.)

The next morning, four accidental tarpon anglers stepped onto a vintage twenty-five-foot wooden panga equipped with a newish, purring eighty-horsepower four stroke. We headed down the Chagres River and into the canal itself, passing ubiquitous and dystopian-looking canal infrastructure: rusting, two-story-tall navigational buoys; dredging derricks; and a lighthouse rising from the rainforest. On the far shore stood a terraced hillside—perhaps scooped out by Teddy Roosevelt himself, who famously insisted on operating a steam shovel for a photo op during construction in 1906.

All the while massive boats pushed impressive wakes that we cleaved through while heading toward Gatun: Death Star–sized containerships that blocked out the sun; rusting bulk carriers; tankers with strange names like *Gaslog Geneva*.

Eventually we banked out of the shipping lanes and eased into a wide bay. In the distance, wisps of low, early morning clouds shrouded the tops of thickly forested, rolling hills. Much of the former Canal Zone is ringed with rainforest intentionally left intact by forward-thinking engineers. Even around 1905, they knew clear-cutting would destabilize watersheds. Since they needed the lake deep and navigable, the forests remained.

The unintended benefit is that today many of those same protected forests are national parks. They swing with monkeys—capuchins, tamarins, howlers—and slow-crawl with sloths. Nearly five hundred bird species, from yellow-throated toucans to mustached antwrens, flutter and flit in the forest canopy.

A long cast off the boat, a pod of mid-sized tarpon rolled, scattering bait. They left behind swirls and eddies that lingered for long seconds before finally breaking up. Then another group rose, this time so close I could hear deep sucking sounds and see golf-ball-sized eyes.

With my ten-weight resting comfortably at home some two thousand miles away, I had a hunch what was coming. Yep, time to troll. The guide passed out banged up spinning gear rigged with seven-inch-long diving plugs and began making slow turns in the panga. I grabbed one and hung on.

A rod went off. Kurt Duchez, a biologist with the Wildlife Conservation Society who usually fights wildlife traffickers, now battled an unseen fish. The rod bucked a few times, but it soon became clear this was no tarpon. A minute later, a bright peacock bass of a few pounds came to the net. Earlier, Duchez showed me images on his phone of a twenty-five-pound mahi mahi he recently caught in his home waters of Guatemala, but he still beamed like a kid as he held the colorful peacock—his first ever.

We continued to troll past rolling tarpon, but nothing happened. So I asked the guide if we could cast topwater plugs. We swapped out deep divers for poppers and sputtered them back to the boat. But the fish were mercurial, coming up over here, and then back over there, and then a hundred feet from where your lure just landed. All the while, I imagined a well-cast Tarpon Toad would have gotten crushed.

We drifted along casting and casting. At one point, the only sound was the gurgling of poppers backdropped with the guttural, raspy calls of black howler monkeys from a nearby island. Meanwhile tarpon porpoised, gulped, and chased. But mostly, they ignored.

Except for one.

Three feet off the boat, five feet of tarpon exploded on my lure flashing a lattice of scales. But then, nothing. It missed and was not coming back.

I stood there for a few moments letting images and audio burn into the dark hard drive where phantoms of lost fish metastasize. Fly rod or no fly rod, this one hurt. A hunch told me it would be our lone tarpon of the morning, and it turned out I was right. The sun rose higher, and the fish stopped working. The Central American heat slowly wilted us until we all agreed it was time to reel up and head back to the dock.

The guide started the motor, which gurgled quietly as he stowed gear for the ride back to the dock. A howler roared in the distance. In front of us, a nine-hundred-foot container ship named *NYK Romulus* out of Singapore lumbered past on its way to the Atlantic.

SOME CASTS IN
GATED FLORIDA

SOME ANGLERS PLAN TRIPS TO FLORIDA YEARS IN ADVANCE, booking top guides or sleek charters during choice dates. Others, visiting family on a last-minute whim, toss a travel rod in their carry-on bag and hope for the best. That was me.

I spotted it from the balcony of my snowbird parents' fourth-floor rented condo: a wadable five-acre tidal flat, a mosaic of swaying turtle grass and sandy marl bordered by a meandering bayou. Somehow it had escaped the developers and subsequent draining, bulkheading, and paving that dominates so much of western Florida. When I pointed the flat out to my octogenarian mom and dad, they nodded, smiled, and turned up Tony Bennett crooning "The Good Life."

That afternoon, spinning rod in hand, I walked behind the pickleball court and heated pool to a manicured path that led to a gap in some mangroves. I hid my shoes and stepped into the Gulf. Sand squished between my toes, and warm saltwater caressed my knees.

Mangroves quickly gave way to knee-deep flats. Offshore, a pelican crash-landed pouch first into the water, then looked around as if hoping no one saw it. A mullet leapt impossibly high and far just because it could.

I began working a Spook, its rhythmic "chik-chik-chik" carrying over a breeze ruffling the surface. With each successive cast, the gated development with its assorted amenities faded behind me into nothingness.

The tourism board calls this region of western Florida the "Sun Coast," claiming it gets more sunny days than anywhere else in the state. Apparently, the sales pitch worked; it's booming here. On my ride from the airport, an endless clutter of strip malls, chain restaurants, and traffic stretched to the horizon.

But look closely, and you can still find vestiges of a primeval Florida still tenaciously hanging on. White ibis probe for insects along the shoulders of highways. Osprey chirp over the drone of leaf blowers. Patches of remnant mangroves lower their roots spider-like, attempting to reclaim what was once theirs.

A wake appeared behind my Spook. I tensed and kept reeling. Then: chik-chik-chik-SWOOSH. I came tight and a redfish slapped its tail in two feet of water, then bored away in second gear. In a few minutes, it surrendered to a lip grabber. Four pounds. Solid slot fish. A quick text to my parents confirmed: "YES—BRING HOME FOR DINNER!" I tethered the locked grabber to a submerged mangrove root with the redfish attached. I went back to casting.

The late afternoon light softened. A frisbee-sized stingray approached my legs then bolted off with exaggerated wing flaps. I fished the Spook with purpose and hope. With a keeper red already in the larder, anything else would be like after-dinner port and a cigar—welcome but unnecessary.

Crash. Something freight-trained the Spook, tore off thirty feet of line then tail-walked out of the water. The hooks held, prompting another jump. Nice snook. The fish ran a second time, heading for a patch of emergent spartina grass. We both wrestled for a few tense moments before the fish yielded. Then it was a matter of steering it within reach, dodging barbless trebles, and lipping it.

It was not huge—maybe twenty-six inches—but it couldn't have given me much more. I found myself cooing at it, letting it bite down on my thumb to let me know it was ready for its release. When I eased my grip, it ghosted toward a depression in the marl and vanished.

Maybe an hour of prime fishing time remained, but I knew my parents were sitting on the balcony watching the sun go down and waiting for their son to return with a redfish.

I waded ashore, put on my shoes, and headed back up the path. A group in Building 3 enjoying their first (or maybe second) cocktail asked from their balcony in a distinctly New York accent: "Hey! What kinda fish is *that*?" When I told them, they seemed astonished such a wild creature could live so close by.

In golden light, I entered my parents' building and felt a blast of air conditioning. I pushed the elevator button dripping a little Gulf water on the faux marble tile. Maybe one hundred feet away, the tide neared its ebb.

A SINGULAR RED

IN THE BAYOUS OF SOUTHEAST LOUISIANA, THERE'S AN OLD-school redfish camp called Bourgeois, where the gastronomic influence of New Orleans hangs like Spanish moss. Lean in, and you'll hear the Cajun guides bantering about tides and flies in one breath, and in the next, how to cook frog's legs by deglazing your pan with bourbon.

I came here, however, not interested in cuisine, but to flyfish for tailing redfish, which, when conditions are right, is the technique-of-choice in this seemingly endless network of marshy islands and shallow passes that stretch to the horizon.

Alas, the weather gods snookered us. The night before, the jagged blue edge of a cold front had descended, and temperatures plummeted into the low forties. By daybreak, northwest winds scudded across the flats, churning and muddying waters.

I stood in a bay boat with a twenty-five-knot headwind slapping my face. Roiled waters swirled everywhere. My eight-weight fly rod sat in a tube in the forward hold. I could string it up, then grunt and groan ineffective casts and otherwise howl at the moon. Or I could try to get a redfish in the boat.

I made my decision. Reluctantly, I reached for the classic Gulf Coast bait rig—a dead shrimp under a popping cork—and spent the next few hours lobbing out sloppy end-over-end casts. Finally, the reel locked up, and the rod bucked violently. Something ripped the surface flashing copper—a solid red, and it pulled like a mule. The beefy thirty-incher I eventually scooped up went into the fish box. By then the tide was almost done. A few minutes later we headed in. Tired and windburned, I watched the marshes zip past. My Louisiana redfish adventure had ended.

Or so I thought.

Back at the dock, I noticed that my fish, along with a couple of slot reds and some speckled trout caught by the other boats, were quickly filleted, bagged, and handed off to an affable fellow in a crisp fishing shirt. He hurried them into a cooler and drove away.

At 5:00 p.m. sharp, ten guests from the lodge stepped onto a chartered bus, and a half hour later we walked into Bourbon House, a stunning restaurant in the heart of New Orleans.

Greeting us was the man in the fishing shirt, now wearing a sport jacket. It was none other than Dickie Brennan, the restaurant's owner and royalty of the New Orleans food scene. A few minutes later, now with cocktails in hand, we followed him into the kitchen where his executive chef awaited to tell us how our catches would be prepared. Over a plateful of fried oyster appetizers and smoked redfish pâté, we learned about making a roux from fish bones and scoring whole fish so they cooked evenly.

The whole thing felt surreal, but it was part of a conservation partnership between restaurants and fishing lodges called "Catch and Cook." The idea is that guests would rather keep one or maybe two fish for a fine meal than fill a cooler with a limit, only to toss freezer-burned fillets into the trash a year later.

I lifted a forkful of "redfish on the half shell," served with crabmeat, and, in my newly acquired New Orleans parlance: "frisée, caramelized balsamic onions, and lemon beurre blanc." Taste buds I never knew existed fired synapses of delight. Fly rod or no fly rod, never had a redfish I caught been honored in such a singular way.

PHONELESS ON A FLAT

IT DIED RIGHT THERE IN MY HANDS, MY ANCIENT BUT TRUST-worthy iPhone SE. I had just stood up from releasing a decent bonefish from a flat on Great Inagua Island in the Bahamas and realized the phone was still in my pants pocket—not in the water-proof pouch in my backpack. A quick check for vitals revealed it was DOA. Cause of death: drowning.

After an initial spaz out, I calmed. When we got back to the guest house, I borrowed my friend Blair's phone and sent a quick text back home explaining what happened and how I would be offline for the rest of the week. Then I opened a Kalik, took a sip, and breathed sultry Bahamian air. Palms rustled overhead. A hummingbird known as an Inagua woodstar hovered around a flowering shrub a few feet away, and I watched its brilliant violet throat patch glinting in the late afternoon sun. Normally, I would have instinctively reached for my phone to grab a few seconds of crappy video. Now, all I could do was observe this tiny, stunning bird buzzing and feeding. I found myself smiling. The woodstar eventually zoomed off. I took another sip and breathed again, this time deeper.

The next day, we slowly scanned an oceanside flat looking for more bones. Seeing nothing, we changed tactics. I rigged for barracuda and wandered south. Blair walked north looking for triggerfish that sometimes surfed the flat's gentle breakers.

I rounded a point and stood on a limestone outcrop just as a decent barracuda glided within range. I got off a cast, and a second later the fish intercepted, lurching the rod in the first of several long runs. After a time, it began to flag, as barracudas do, and I drew it closer. With no phone, there was never that moment of mental gymnastics figuring out how to get ready for a photo op, or thinking about some clever phrasing to concoct for my social media feed (though "torpedo w/fins" briefly came to mind). Instead, I remained focused and present, eventually using a wave to guide the estimated twenty-pound fish into the shallows. The barracuda was muscular and toothy with an azure back and sooty blotches on its belly. I let it go, and the visual of it swimming off now belongs only to me.

Beyond the reef crest, impossibly blue, cerulean water stretched to the horizon. Pre-phone dunking, I may have felt the need to take an image or two that I would look at later and delete because it failed to truly capture this almost surreal color. Now, unshackled, I stood, stared, and absorbed. I pondered the word *cerulean* and how beautiful it sounds. I said it out loud just so I could hear it: "Cerulean." I felt like Morgan Freeman reciting "Zihuatanejo" in *The Shawshank Redemption*. If I still had my phone, by now, I probably would have been scrolling to see how many people liked my barracuda post.

On our penultimate day, on the advice of our host, we hiked to the strangest tarpon spot I had ever fished. It was a half-acre tannin-stained pond excavated long ago for gravel and sand. Bahamian scrub had since reclaimed it, and somewhere along the way tarpon colonized. How they lived out their lives and whether they had access to other waters via an underwater cave or portal remained a mystery. All I know is that, when we approached, several fish rolled and blurped flashing silver. We both cast. Blair missed one on a Toad, and I blew a take on a Gummy Minnow when I trout set. Then the pond went quiet.

Blair eventually decided to head back to the truck, but I wanted to try one more fly. I tied on a smallish Tabory's Snake Fly in lime green—a sneaky pattern with a spun deer hair head, marabou body, and tail of undulating ostrich herl and just enough flash. I cast and gave it a slow, erratic retrieve, shucking and jiving it through the pond. A tarpon took it down in a swirl. This time, I strip-set and watched the fish jump again and again. In "baby tarpon" vernacular, it was still in diapers, weighing maybe five pounds. When I eventually slid it in the shallows, it stared back with its oversize silver dollar eye, flanks bronzed from a life well lived in tannin. The bright snake eel hung from its scoop-like maw. It was a lovely image.

No pics, though; you'll have to take my word for it.

A Char by
Any Other Name

The plan was solid: travel to the Canadian Rockies for a weeklong vacation with my family. Hike mountains; marvel at glaciers and alpine lakes. See elk, moose, and maybe a grizzly bear or two. Then—and only then—make some side casts for westslope cutthroat, or try to catch my first-ever bull trout, the large, predatory char native to these wild mountain rivers.

But stuff happened. When we landed in Calgary, wildfires in northern British Columbia and southern Alberta shrouded the front-range in a grayish haze. The fires, I learned, were exacerbated by the mountain pine beetle, now colonizing at ever-higher elevations due to milder winters. They leave behind skeletal forests of brown tinder—a lightning strike away from pyrotechnics. On top of that, an unusually warm July caused runoff—lots of runoff—to gush from glaciers clogging most larger rivers with rock flour. Thanks, climate change.

On the third day, the wind shifted, and the smoke retreated. By day six, we completed most of our hikes and saw many of the requisite wildlife, highlighted by a minivan-sized bull moose browsing along a lake, and a sow griz with cubs spotted from the safety of the rental car. Now, with family satiated and resting for the afternoon, it was time to cast.

I drove beside a non-glacial, clearwater stream that tumbled and twisted in and out of view. From the road, the scene looked like something out of a Bob Ross painting: craggy peaks looming in the distance, foothills dark with spruce, the stream a titanium-white brush stroke of rushing water.

I pulled into a turnoff, tugged on waders, and strung up my five-weight. Next to my wading staff, I holstered a can of bear spray, making me feel both badass and scared shitless. Then, repeating a singsong "HEY-BEAR-HEY-MOOSE," I loped down a game trail until I came to the stream. Warblers flitted from bankside willows snatching mayfly duns in mid-flight. Good sign. Upriver I saw the first fishable spot, a juicy thigh-deep run that eddied along an undercut bank.

Looking back now, I felt almost cocky as I stripped off a few arm lengths of line. A friendly tailwind took my hair-wing spider and placed it two inches off the bank into a bubble line, thank you very much. I tensed for what was about to happen. The fly bobbed along. I tensed some more. Any second now. Any. Second. But the fly traveled the entire length of the pool without so much as a swirl or flash. I made another cast. Same result. Inconceivable. On a mountain stream like this, six trout should have battled over who gets first slash. I made one last swing and whiffed again. A chunk of confidence calved off my psyche and melted.

The next run, similar in its comeliness, produced more of the same. I could feel myself speeding up my casting to cover more water. Desperation seeped into my drifts.

I approached one more bend and decided that this would be my pool to die on. Here, the flow deepened then shouldered against a logjam. Bleached roots spiderwebbed below the surface. A gap between two toppled spruce boughs screamed out as the pool's clear sweet spot. With the right cast, a well-mended fly would get a good yard of drag-free float, which was all you would need. If nothing moved, then this otherwise perfect-looking stream must be a mirage.

I cast, and once again a magical breeze took the wheel and punched the fly deep into the opening. The spider stood on its end, twerked, and was engulfed. I lifted with joy and wrestled a trout from the refuge of the branches. When I saw flashes of salmon and yellow, I thought at first it was a cutthroat. But then I could make out the cream-tipped pectoral fins of a char. My first native bull trout? The fish thrashed on the surface showing more color. Nope. Brook trout. Seconds later, a lovely twelve-inch brookie hung in my net. A char, yes, but native, no. The brook trout's natural range ends in northeastern Manitoba about a thousand miles from where I stood.

The brookie, progeny of some long-ago stocking, rested in my partially submerged net. I considered this fish, which had just risen from beneath a logjam to eat my floating fly. It may not have been a native bull trout or cutthroat, but it was as wild as the introduced rainbows and browns I happily catch in my home waters back east—waters that, ironically, used to contain only native brook trout. I dipped the net and watched the trout swim to a bowling-ball-sized rock midstream where it held in the current. A warbler caught my eye for a few seconds. When I looked back at the fish, it had vanished.

The next day, I met up with a local fishing guide for a quick beer. I told him about the trout, and he seemed genuinely surprised. He explained that, downstream, a slot canyon with a series of waterfalls prevents any upriver migration, and a lake several miles upriver has no outlet except for a series of intermittent underwater caves. He told me that until now, he had never heard of any trout caught in that section of the stream. I nodded and sipped my beer.

No one told the trout. No one told me. Always make the cast.

Faith and Time
and Atlantic Salmon

Consistent success in Atlantic salmon fishing requires an abundance of one of two things: either money—to be whisked away to Iceland or Labrador or some other far-flung place where fish still outnumber anglers—or time—to camp out on a salmon river and fish for weeks on end. Anglers with neither at their disposal should expect encounters with the "fish of kings" to come along about as frequently as a solar eclipse.

For those who regularly fish the gentle Margaree River on Cape Breton Island, time seems to be the common asset, with many local anglers "taking a pass" through their favorite salmon pool as part of their daily routines.

Bob Carpenter is one of them. A former West Coast commercial fisherman, he retired in the early 1980s at age thirty-eight, thanks to some smart real estate investments. Since then, he fishes for salmon about one hundred days a year.

Bob was there when I caught my one and only Atlantic salmon in the Margaree's famous Seal Pool a few years earlier. He tailed the fish for me, a bright nine-pound male, then shook my hand, making me feel as if I had just been admitted into a secret society.

When he called recently, explaining that a wet spring had set the stage for what may be the Margaree's best run in a decade, I planned a trip for later in the month, thinking I had locked into a sure thing.

But a lot can happen on a salmon river over the course of a few weeks. For example, it can stop raining and get really hot—two things that shut down runs as matter-of-factly as turning off a spigot. Atlantic salmon use rivers like watery highways to reach their spawning grounds; not enough flow keeps them idling in estuaries for weeks.

When Bob met me at the airport, he wore the ever-optimistic smile of the hard-core salmon angler. "We could use a little rain," was all he said.

That night, while sitting in his house overlooking the Gulf of Saint Lawrence, he showed me photo after photo of salmon and salmon anglers. Most were of the Margaree regulars cradling beautiful, chrome-sided fish—a fifteen-pounder taken by Robert Chiasson on a dry fly last year, a thirty-pounder landed by Henry Green a few years before that. Every image came with its own story, and Bob could remember the most minute details including fly patterns, time of day, how many times the fish jumped. Among salmon anglers, each fish remains a singular event; it is clearly not a numbers game.

The next morning we woke before dawn. Humid, still air held the faint promise of rain as we drove to the river. By sunrise, we sat on a bench overlooking the Seal Pool, awaiting 6:00 a.m., the legal time to begin fishing.

Throughout the Margaree, benches built by local fishing guides can be seen along the banks of the more popular pools. These benches not only allow anglers to rest between passes but also facilitate the wonderful Nova Scotia tradition of "rotating pools," where anglers begin at the head, cast, take two steps, and cast again until all the water is covered. Done right, groups of anglers can all fish at the same time, getting equal shots at the best lies. If the pool gets too crowded, anglers wait their turn on the benches. Bob called the bench at Seal Pool "the batting cage."

Patrick Mahoney, a friend of Bob's, soon emerged from the far bank, waded across the river, and joined us at the bench. Patrick recently moved from Halifax to a house that he had built just downriver, so he could fish every day. He sat with us and spoke of a nice salmon he lost the week before.

"It came up right there," Mahoney said, pointing to a gentle eddy swirling behind a submerged boulder. "Took my fly and broke off when I set the hook. Helluva nice fish."

Bob quickly pointed out that more fish are caught on the Seal Pool bench than anywhere on the river.

At precisely 6:01 a.m. we began our rotation, making long casts to the prime lies against the far bank. Though low water and warm weather had clearly put the fish out of a "taking" mood, Bob and Patrick fished with the boundless patience, fueled by faith, that drives all seasoned salmon fishermen.

Admittedly, I became impatient. After several passes through the pool, I decided to cross the river to a high bank that might allow at least a glimpse of a fish or two.

When I reached the other side, I cautiously approached a deep drop-off, peering into the river with polarized glasses. A window of current flowed past, giving a sudden clear view of four ten-pound Atlantic salmon swimming so close to each other they could touch.

I called out to Bob and Patrick that fish held just off the bank from where I stood. Then I watched as they each took turns putting perfectly timed casts over the lie. But if salmon could ever look indifferent or even apathetic, these four fish had it mastered. After another hour of casting, we broke down our rods and took a long break for lunch.

When we returned to the river in the late afternoon, I headed directly for the high bank to see if the four salmon remained in the lie. A half dozen four-to-six-pound shad held there instead.

The fish swam nervously, periodically chasing each other into the shallows, unleashing pent-up bursts of speed. Shad range throughout Nova Scotia but remain largely ignored—especially by salmon fishermen.

"Shad," I excitedly called out, pointing to the lie. "They'll hit a bright fly if you put it in front of them."

Patrick and Bob stared at me with nearly the same expression as the salmon from earlier that morning. I might as well have proposed using a gillnet to catch carp.

Maybe not, I thought.

Eventually Bob headed home, while Patrick agreed to take me upriver to another pool where a few fish had been spotted the day before. We drove through the broad Margaree valley glimpsing quiet pools with empty benches overlooking them. By early evening, we were casting again, this time through a series of faster runs that Patrick described as good taking pools.

I worked the upper run, while Patrick chose the lower pool. He eventually waded around the bend until I could no longer see him. Though I covered the water thoroughly with a battery of both wet and dry flies, no fish rose.

Another salmon fisherman—one of the few seen that hot day— came from upriver and took a leisurely pass at the pool. He methodically fished a wet fly down and across the current, letting it swim for a few seconds at the end of each cast, before picking it up with a sweep of his rod, and sending it a few feet farther downstream.

Beyond him the sun had dipped below a forested hill, and a few wispy clouds turned from gold, to orange, to pink. Two veeries sang from opposite sides of the river, their rolling, metallic calls echoing from bank to bank above the water's gentle hiss.

When he reached the bottom of the run, he reeled in his line and headed up the bank, stopping in front of me. "Lovely spot, isn't it?" he said in his faint Cape Breton brogue. He wore a weathered cap that covered silver hair, and his vest, waders, and tackle all had the well-worn, comfortable feel of a broken-in baseball glove.

"Fish are like icing on the cake here," he said. "It's nice to have them, but it's just as nice to be here."

He surveyed the river and nearby woods for a short time before saying goodbye. Then I watched him proceed up the bank and eventually out of sight, walking with the contented gait that all Margaree fishermen seem to have. Clearly he would fish again the next day, and the one after that.

PILE OF FISH

Wow did Big Joe love to fish! And was he good at it! Really good! He would beat you to the cast like a gunslinger outdrawing you with his six-shooter. While you were midway through a double haul, Big Joe would fire out a lure with his spinning rod that would land inches from a rolling silver salmon. A couple of turns and he would rear back with a mighty hook set. Then he'd turn to you and ask if you wanted to reel it in.

Here's the problem: Big Joe was a fishing guide. Another problem: I had just hired him for five days of fishing in Alaska.

Some anglers are "guide guys"; they wouldn't dream of traveling anywhere exotic without booking a pro to take them around. I get that; it's smart, but it's not me. I prefer to work the problem on my own. That's how I caught my first bonefish, tarpon, and Atlantic salmon. Yes, there were steep learning curves involved and sometimes lots of frustration. But in the end, I hooked, fought, and landed those fish myself, by God.

When I started researching DIY fishing for my first trip to Alaska, it sounded different. Much of what I read warned about Alaska's limited road system and inevitable combat fishing. Images of rivers and streams overrun with anglers resembled opening day of trout season in New Jersey, except with snow-capped mountains in the background. If you decided to attempt a more adventurous wilderness experience and hike into the bush on your own, one bad decision and a grizzly bear would swat your ass into beef medallions. It seemed foolhardy not to hire a guide.

On the recommendation of a friend of a friend, my wife, Mimi, and I wound up choosing a fishing package on a big Alaskan river that boasted five species of salmon, plus enormous rainbows, char, and grayling. It sounded perfect; our guide, Big Joe, would pick us up each day after breakfast in his boat, then whisk us away to unlimited boat and wade fishing in America's last frontier. Before I booked the trip, I even had the all-important client-guide conversation where I explained that I wanted to catch my first-ever silver salmon on my fly rod. "No problem," he told me over the phone.

We met Big Joe at the dock, and he lived up to his name, standing a good six feet five and weighing north of 250 pounds. Camo neoprene waders, military moustache, and a well-worn Cabela's baseball hat completed his burly Alaskan look.

He fired up the boat, and we took our seats. I noticed an arsenal of tackle already on board—several spinning rods and a fly rod or two. We had brought our own gear, so I assumed they must be backups just in case I splintered a rod on a big salmon.

Anticipation ran high as we motored downriver through blue-green waters. In the distance, snowy peaks from some faraway mountain range hung low on the horizon. "We're going to find a pile of fish," Big Joe said over the outboard. Then he added for emphasis: "A pile of fish."

The boat slowed, and we spotted a few swirls from salmon that had just entered from saltwater. The boat, a sixteen-foot aluminum deep-V, seemed tight for two fly anglers plus a guide, so Mimi opted to spinfish, casting a bright marabou jig from amidships. I took the bow and had just started stripping off fly line from my reel, when I heard the whizz of another cast from the back of the boat. I turned around and saw Big Joe fishing.

Admittedly, I wasn't all that versed in guide etiquette, but I did know one cardinal rule: a guide should never fish unless specifically invited by their clients. And even then, only for brief demonstration purposes, such as showing proper drift speed or line mending, or something else technical. This is for obvious reasons—namely, so the clients, not the guide, catch the fish. It should not bear repeating, but I will do so anyway—the guide is being *paid* to put *clients* on the fish, *not catch the fish themselves*.

Seconds later, this all became moot. "I got one!" Joe yelled. Yep, the very first salmon of our Alaskan adventure went to Big Joe. A few casts later, so did the second.

"Cast over there," Joe excitedly said, clearly in the zone. "There's a pile of fish."

A silver rolled thirty feet off the boat. I picked up my line to make a cast, but before I could shoot the fly, Joe's lure got there first. He hooked another salmon. And that's when he turned to me and said: "You want to reel this one in?"

So utterly gobsmacked was I, and facing down the fact that I would spend the next five days in a boat with him; and not sure I could answer my brawny, mustachioed fishing guide without screaming *"Are you fucking kidding me???"* I just swallowed and said, "No."

Okay—some of you at this point may be saying, "What the hell is the matter with you—you should have said something. You're paying him!" And you are right; looking back, there were probably lots of ways I could have approached Big Joe and told him—in the nicest of ways—to cut the shit. But I didn't, and I have to live with that. Maybe it's because I'm too much of a gentleman. Did I mention that Joe was a big and excitable fella?

Let's go back to the scene continuing to unfold on the boat. After Joe's third salmon, I had somehow twisted my fly line into a truly awful knot that forced me to pop off my spool and snake line in and out of the reel frame to untangle it. A long time passed without me making a single cast. By now, the fishing slowed. Big Joe, perhaps bored from temporarily not catching fish, decided then—and only then—to ask if I needed help.

This time my answer was a louder and more emphatic "*No.*" Mimi looked at me, not fully understanding the nuclear war going on in my head. The rest of the day is admittedly a little fuzzy. I know we caught salmon—mostly pinks, which far outnumbered the silvers.

Back at our hotel, I sucked down Alaskan Ambers and hated on Big Joe.

The next day, Joe motored us up a slow tributary. We got out of the boat and hiked a few hundred yards through knee-deep water to a sluggish pool full of ambivalent silvers that wouldn't hit. I noticed that Big Joe didn't bring a rod—a tip-off that the fishing might not be so good here. After an hour of nothing, with the feeling that Joe might keep us here a while to kill some time, I asked him if he wouldn't mind going back to the boat to bring us our bug spray. The blackflies were pretty bad, I told him. He made it clear he did mind, stomping through the river like an angry giant. He came back with the bug spray. I thanked him and put it in my pocket. Maybe I would put it on later, I told him. It was playing passive-aggressive chess. Your move, Big Joe.

It took my wife, all five feet, three inches of her, to finally stand up to Big Joe. On day 3, Joe motored us upriver and beached the boat above a long series of riffles and runs. He grabbed his own fly rod and, gesturing at the river, said, "Pile of fish out here." Then he disappeared around the bend.

We fished for a while, catching a few more pinks and some char. I briefly hooked an enormous colored-up, but out-of-season, king salmon that went airborne and easily broke off. Eventually, Mimi waded around the bend where she found Big Joe resting on a rock.

"Catch any, Joe?" she asked.

Joe took in a deep, satisfied breath then proceeded to proudly list the dozens of fish he had just landed: grayling, char, silvers, pinks, even an eight-pound rainbow, which would have been the fish of the trip for either of us.

Mimi stood silent for a moment then said: "Wow, Joe, did you leave us any?"

"Oh . . . sure," Joe stammered. "There's still . . . a . . . a . . . pile of fish out there . . . a pile . . ."

Mimi walked away before he could finish.

After that, Joe became quiet, you might even say sullen. Defanged, he never made another cast. For the next two days, he put us on more fish, and we caught them. And I recall some genuine highlights: lovely grayling rising to mayflies in riffles, intercepting a twenty-inch rainbow that was chasing down salmon smolts like a bonito. But again, much of the trip has gotten fuzzy. For me, Big Joe could never recover from his original etiquette breach. It was like a loud fart at the beginning of a first date—no matter what happens afterward, no matter how good the meal may have been or how wonderful the movie you just saw, what you remember most is the stink.

On the last day, Joe drove us to the airport. I gave him his tip, which was not a dollar more than adequate, and we boarded our plane. Yeah, I know, but I don't have it in me to be a crappy tipper or to stiff him outright. Call it a character flaw.

And as for Big Joe. . . . To paraphrase from the ending of one of my favorite movies, *The Road Warrior*: "That was the last we ever saw of him. He lives now . . . only in my nightmares."

Two years later, Mimi and I opted to take our chances on Alaska's road system and found something far more practical than Big Joe—a beater rental car with a cracked windshield, leaky gas tank, and a laminated piece of paper taped to the glove box that read: "Do not put salmon on the back seat."

We parked the car at the end of a pitted dirt road and hiked along a boardwalk through some muskeg. It ended where a clearwater stream flowed into an estuary. Salmon rolled everywhere. We shared the spot with a few bald eagles and a lone seal, but no one else. And yeah, we caught a pile of fish.

Discovering Limits
on an Alaskan Stream

The massive, stark face of Scott Glacier loomed in the distance as my friend Jim Leedom battled yet another silver salmon. Downstream, Dave Taft had one on, too. A moment later my own fly came to an abrupt halt midriver. I stripped to set the hook, and a bright ten-pound male wallowed, churned, and heaved in the current. It was our eighth fish in a half hour—or maybe our ninth. At that point, we had already lost count.

Glaciers, grizzly bears, and moose notwithstanding, Alaskan salmon fishing sometimes feels a little like Montauk in October, with hordes of migrating fish pouncing on your flies like blitzing bluefish or marauding stripers. Time your trip right—in this case early autumn for gregarious silver salmon—and the rivers may run black with shoals of spawning fish.

Unlike the more celebrated Atlantic salmon, whose scarcity and moodiness in taking a fly has resulted in elegant but rigid traditions, fishing for silvers here along Prince William Sound has a far more relaxed feel. Local people and visiting anglers frequently share the same pools, casting side by side as dogs bark, youngsters squeal, and fish flop on the bank. Visitors also quickly learn that fishing success is not measured in vague "rises," or missed fish, as it is with Atlantic salmon but, rather, the hard currency of pounds and filling one's limit.

In an increasingly catch-and-release world where decked-out fly-fishers coddle their fish before releasing them, it is admittedly refreshing to see a guy in hip boots and a Harley Davidson hat haul a fish ashore with a heavy spinning rod and knock it on the head for dinner.

Jim and Dave, both of whom I've watched tenderly revive Catskill trout caught on barbless flies, quickly slipped into fillet-and-release mode. After each of them landed their salmon, they jabbed them through the gills with pieces of driftwood and carried them caveman style back to the car.

By the end of our weeklong trip, we had diligently filled our daily limits—three fish for each angler—and released dozens more. Our shoulders ached from battling silver after silver, and our hands were raw with line burns and bite marks from particularly toothy specimens.

So we decided to scale down our tackle and spend the rest of the day trying for the far less taxing Dolly Varden, a member of the char family and close cousin to the brook trout.

Named after a Charles Dickens character who wore gaudy costumes in the novel *Barnaby Rudge*, dollies—and particularly males in their fall spawning colors—make even the most vivid brookie appear downright drab. Teal flanks covered with vermilion polka dots, peach bellies, ivory-tipped fins, and a charcoal-splashed head look as if they were conjured by a five-year-old experimenting with a new box of crayons.

Dollies follow schools of silvers from saltwater into rivers, often holding behind spawning fish where they gobble dislodged eggs from nests. Eventually they scavenge on the spawned-out remains of the salmon, too.

We wandered along the treeless, serpentine banks of a small salmon river until we found a submerged gravel bar that dropped off to a deep undercut bank—a perfect spot for both silvers and dollies. Sure enough, a few salmon could be seen holding in the current—bright, heavy-bodied fish as long as your arm. Beneath them, ghostlike, flashed a pack of smaller dollies.

Matching the hatch consisted of tying on an Iliamna Pinky—nothing more than a ball of pink chenille wrapped around a weighted, short-shank hook. When they are flipped up current with a few split shot, they roll along the bottom and mimic a salmon egg perfectly.

I made the first cast and watched a small Dolly Varden immediately dart out and grab the fly. Unceremoniously, I hauled the twelve-incher Huck Finn style up the bank, where I quickly unhooked it and dropped it back into the river.

A minute later, Jim and Dave both landed slightly larger fish. It all seemed comfortably familiar, as if we were nymphing for trout back home.

After each of us caught and released a few more dollies, two salmon fishermen began cleaning their catch along the bank upstream, sending a steady plume of offal to the undercut bank where the fish held. Small bits of flesh and salmon roe settled to the bottom.

Dozens of dollies began racing this way and that, grabbing pieces of flesh and gobs of roe like bluefish tearing through a chum-slick. Even the salmon responded, driven by instincts known only to their own kind. One particularly large silver snatched an entire skein of roe, then swam around with it like a dog with a chew toy before eventually letting it go.

I quickly changed to a flesh fly—a knot of salmon-colored rabbit fur—and began splattering it up current and letting it dead-drift. Larger dollies jumped on it, and I promptly landed two fat sixteen-inchers. These fish wore the same chrome-sided flanks of the silvers, revealing that they, too, had probably just arrived from saltwater.

Jim and Dave did equally well, laughing and clowning as they hooked or missed dollies on nearly every drift. Then a beast of a salmon surprised me and grabbed the fly. I resisted in setting the hook, not wanting my five-weight to blow up in my hands. A few seconds later the big fish gently spit it out—where it was immediately grabbed by another dolly.

After another hour, most of the salmon moved upriver, with the dollies presumably in hot pursuit. Eventually we left the river carrying no dead fish, but with our own limits filled just the same.

PART VIII

FINAL CASTS

Last cast. I promise.

—ME, 1980–PRESENT

Eric's Jetty

I replayed the voicemail one more time just to be sure.

"Steve, it's Eric. I'm dying. Come see me."

Gut punch. Because I knew Eric really was dying. The year before, he had been diagnosed with leukemia, and while initial treatments appeared successful, the awful disease came clawing back. This time, there would be no recovery.

The next day, I drove out to visit him at his home on Long Island.

I had known Eric for ten years. We worked together for the first three. From the beginning, we bonded over a love of fishing. I would tell him stories about fly casting for trout on the Upper Delaware or catching stripers at Sandy Hook. He told me about his college days sneaking out before class to cast for northern pike on swampy creeks in the Adirondacks.

His home water, though, was a jetty on the south shore of Long Island where he often went surfcasting.

Eric connected to the ocean on a much more intimate level than I ever did. Along with fishing, he surfed, snorkeled, and was a scuba diver. At home, he kept a hundred-gallon saltwater reef tank. When I first saw it, bedazzled with bright corals, the tank looked surprisingly devoid of fish. "Most of them are hiding," he told me. "They don't recognize you." He was serious, and I believed him.

We fished together only a few times. Once we met at Montauk Point on a gray morning in October to surfcast for bluefish. Nasty rollers battered the always treacherous rocks below the Montauk lighthouse. I stood far back from the breakers in my studded cleats, waders, and foul weather top, bracing whenever a large wave exploded sending whitewater high in the air. Eric, on the other hand, clambered down to get closer to the action. He wore no waders or cleats, or even raingear, and positioned himself in a gap between two jetty rocks. There, wave after wave pummeled him while he caught bluefish on nearly every cast. He whooped and hollered and looked like Poseidon himself, waving his ten-foot surf rod like a trident. I watched in awe.

When Eric moved on to another job working for an aquarium wholesaler, we saw each other less but stayed in touch. He would sometimes call me with fishing reports. They always began the same way. I'd answer the phone, and with no preamble, no hello, no how's it going, Eric would simply begin: "So I'm on the jetty..." No matter what I was doing; no matter how busy I may have been at work or at home, I would stop everything I was doing and eagerly listen. There was the time the big striper shook off just before he slid it onto the rocks; when he snorkeled off the jetty tip and a school of false albacore blitzed on silversides directly over his head. Some stories were about mystery fish—a missed strike or something mighty that swirled behind a plug but never came back.

Once he told me a terrifying account when he got caught in an electrical storm and was nearly struck by lightning. He made it off the jetty just as the squall hit and turned around to see a lightning bolt strike exactly where he stood casting two minutes earlier. Like so many surfers, Eric was a weather junkie, so that story began with: "So I am on the jetty staring up at a fifty-thousand-foot cumulonimbus..."

His house that day was busy with visitors. Eric's wife told me to go upstairs to the bedroom where some of his friends and coworkers had gathered. All were there for the same reason: to say goodbye.

I walked into the room, and Eric lay in bed. Five or six guys I didn't know were sitting in chairs or standing. I shook each of their hands then gave Eric a hug. He felt warm. One of the friends gave up the chair closest to Eric and invited me to sit. The conversation in the room meandered, and Eric seemed to drift in and out. At one point, two of his coworkers began talking about a new saltwater filtration system coming onto the market. Eric brightened and joined the conversation, saying how much he liked the new filter, and all three started discussing its attributes. For a moment I felt like a visitor in their breakroom, and everything was fine.

But it wasn't. At one point, Eric said with frustration and sadness that he was going to miss out on so many things. Everyone in the room knew he had two boys under five years old who were about to lose their dad. We all fell silent for a few seconds pondering the unthinkable, when one of his friends managed: "Eric, we're all going to the same place eventually. Some of us are going to get there sooner than others."

Eric nodded. He understood. I believe we all did.

Then the time came for me to head home. I wasn't sure what I would say to my friend—the last time I would ever see him in this life. I leaned over and hugged him hard.

"I'll see you on the jetty," I whispered.

He looked at me with a knowing smile and said: "I'll be the big swirl."

Two days later, Eric died. He was thirty-eight.

THE DROWNING

IF APRIL IS THE CRUELEST MONTH, MARCH CAN LAY CLAIM TO the most beguiling. It can lull you into thinking spring has finally arrived, caressing you with a Sunday afternoon in the mid-seventies, only to pelt you with snow and forty-mile-per-hour winds come Monday morning.

It was on one of those sunny and unusually warm March days that I stood on a submerged boulder in the lower Delaware River casting for early season walleye. But I wasn't beguiled; I could see the river was swollen with snowmelt and knew that water temperatures hovered in the low forties. Underneath my waders, I had fortified myself with thick, insulated socks and a layer of fleece thermals. And as I often do early in the season when the river is up and the currents swift, I buckled on a life jacket before I made my first cast. One slip in the Delaware's unforgiving, heavy water could be catastrophic.

The rest of the world treated the day like it was early June. Along a riverwalk behind me, people in shorts and T-shirts sat on benches basking in the sun. Joggers and bicyclists crowded the gravel walking path. I didn't begrudge them; I'd be doing the same if I didn't feel the allure of a heavy pre-spawn walleye lurking somewhere out there in the currents. But so far, an hour's worth of casting had yielded not so much as a bump.

Then something upriver caught my eye. A few hundred yards away, two paddlers made their way downstream in a green canoe. I stopped casting and watched. The scene looked almost surreal—the canoeists taking slow, measured strokes like they were paddling along a duck pond, not a quarter-mile-wide river pushing along at just a few feet below flood stage. Capsize here and frigid river water would numb you into severe hypothermia within minutes or drown you outright. They paddled a little closer, and I noticed neither of them wore life jackets. A pit formed in my stomach. Did they know about the wingdam?

Just above where I fished, a two-hundred-yard-long low-slung, concrete dam jutted into the river. Water rushed over it creating a sort of waterfall that dropped into a cauldron of confused currents that boiled and surged. Though the dam itself was impassable, you could navigate around the far end into a chute of fast water in the center of the river. Below that loomed a series of standing waves from class II and III rapids. To avoid them, you needed to turn hard left as soon as you made it around the end of the dam.

It was a tricky paddle but not impossible. The season before—though a month later in the year and with the river running somewhat lower—I stood in almost the exact spot casting for shad and watched a man and woman in a rowboat approach the dam. The man was shirtless, and the woman wore a bathing suit. Again, no visible life jackets, and I worried they would swamp in the rapids. But the man deftly maneuvered the little rowboat through the chute, leaned into the oars and managed the hard left turn, and eventually paddled past me. The entire time, the woman struck a sunbathing pose on the bow and never moved. I watched them continue downriver and around the next bend. It was impressive seamanship.

This time, however, felt different. For one, the river ran higher and colder. And there was something about the canoeists; they looked oblivious to what the river could unleash. Just then, the paddler in the bow lifted himself from his seat as if to get a better view of something ahead. Then he gestured something with his arms, and the two began paddling frantically to the center of the river. It looked as if they had just noticed the approaching wing-dam for the first time. *Oh shit.*

The next part was both painful and terrifying to watch. They flailed with their paddles attempting to steer around the end of the dam. And they actually made it, but not before a heavy current spun them backwards. The chute of water grabbed the canoe and drove it into the first standing wave pitching it sideways. The second wave rolled them easily. Two heads bobbed next to the green hull. I snapped out of what I was witnessing. I realized I left my phone in my car, so I scrambled up the bank yelling for someone to call 911. Then I ran down the path above the river, where I could see the two bobbing heads and the upside-down green canoe getting swept through more rapids.

Within minutes, I heard sirens, and a police cruiser came tearing up the walking path from downriver. People farther along the path gathered at a trail that led to the water. When I reached them, one of them said a fisherman had just helped a canoeist make it to shore. Then I heard yelling: "Where's my dad? Where's my dad?" The second canoeist hadn't made it out of the river.

I stood there numb. An ambulance arrived, and paramedics helped the son, who looked to be in his mid-twenties, climb inside. In the distance, I heard the growl of an approaching rescue boat searching for the missing canoeist.

I approached a police officer. "I saw what happened," I told her. All at once, the trauma of what I witnessed overwhelmed me, and I found myself sobbing. I said I should have warned the paddlers about the rapids, and I feared the father had drowned. She tried to reassure me that the rescue boat would find him. But I knew that wasn't going to happen—at least not right away. Too much time had passed since the canoe first capsized. I read enough about cold water immersion and hypothermia to understand that, by now, the odds of survival had already diminished to near-zero. She sat me in the police car, where I gave a full statement. Later that night I checked a local news site. Rescuers still hadn't found him.

A few weeks later, I read a news story that the body had been recovered ten miles downriver. He was a fifty-eight-year-old pharmaceutical engineer from Princeton out for an afternoon paddle with his son. They had canoed for a few miles along the canal that runs parallel to the Delaware. On a whim—and because it was such a warm and beautiful day—they decided to launch in the swollen river and paddle back to their car downstream.

I kept playing through my mind what I could have done. Maybe when I first saw the canoeists, I could have run up the riverbank above the dam and screamed for them to turn around. But I also knew that even when I first saw them, they had probably already reached a point of no return. I've sometimes imagined that I see them at the launch ramp just before they put their canoe in the river and I talk them out of the trip altogether. It's a nice fleeting thought.

Instead, more than a decade later, I find myself as sort of self-appointed lifeguard at this still dangerous but productive fishing spot. Early in the season when the walleye and shad fishing can be excellent—particularly at the frothing end of the dam—I tell anglers they should wear life jackets and, in the same breath, mention the drowning. Whenever I get to the second part, the conversation immediately turns serious. Maybe it's working because each season I see more anglers wearing them.

Last spring, I watched a kayaker preparing to launch below the wingdam. He was readying his gear when I noticed he wasn't wearing a life jacket. I approached and asked if he had one. He kind of looked me over and told me yes, it was stored in a hatch behind him. I suggested he should wear it, explaining one more time about the drowning I witnessed here.

His expression changed. "No shit?" he said. He reached into the hatch, pulled out the life jacket and shrugged it on, then clicked it tight. "I appreciate it," he told me, before shoving off into the river. I watched him paddle downstream until he was out of sight.

THE GHOST OF DAVE PALMER

No one fished with more intensity than my friend Dave Palmer. When he suited up in his camouflage waders and drew out his rod, he transformed into a great blue heron, or maybe a Navy SEAL. His posture lowered, and he would creep and stalk and patiently wait out his prey.

No one I knew could spot fish better either. I remember when he picked out a steelhead holding beneath bubbles and heavy current on a Lake Ontario tributary.

"It's right there," he said, pointing at nothing but bubbles and current.

"Where? *Where*??" I demanded.

Just then, the faintest outline of a thirty-inch wild steelhead ghosted into view before dissolving back into rushing water. Ninety-nine out of one hundred anglers would have walked right past it.

"Dave, how the hell did you see that?" I asked.

He remained silent, not dignifying my stupid question with an answer.

There is a cliché about thinking like a fish, but Dave could actually do it. He once took me to a reservoir full of large hybrid striped bass where the best fishing took place well after midnight. Every few minutes, hungry hybrids crashed schools of alewives spawning noisily in the shallows.

When I first heard the violent breaks from feeding stripers, I said to myself, *this will be easy.* I'll cast out a surface lure, chug it a few times, and hook one. But I quickly learned those hybrids had earned their PhDs. With so many thousands of spawning alewives around them, they would hold back, then all at once gang-rush the schools in blitzes that lasted seconds. Cast after cast went ignored.

Meanwhile, a hundred feet away, Dave stood motionless and silent. I could make out his shadowy outline in the darkness and see the glow of his cigarette waxing and waning with each drag. Then at some trigger point known only to Dave, I heard the whirr of his baitcasting reel followed by the plunk of a surface plug. After a single twitch, a cinderblock in the form of a large hybrid depth-charged his lure. I heard Dave rear back to set the hook followed by a low laugh. He had won the chess match.

Later he explained to me that he figured out the cadence of the spawning alewives just before the hybrids charged in. He knew just when the bass were about to pounce and timed his cast accordingly. Like I said, the man thought like a fish.

Dave taught fly casting on the side, and when my wife expressed interest in learning how to fly-fish, I smartly hired Dave to give her lessons. All these years later, her double haul remains textbook.

But then Dave got sick and wound up in the hospital. Something to do with his liver. Though I knew he had been sober for years, he once told me he lived hard during his former days as a biker. He was admitted the day before I was leaving on a trip to Yellowstone with my wife. I called him, and he spoke to me from his hospital bed. As I expected, he first gave me some advice on fly patterns and places to fish in the park. Then he said, "Visit me when you get back. And don't get freaked out that I look yellow."

A few days into the trip we parked at a turnout that overlooked lower Slough Creek. We had spent a fine day catching wild cutthroats, so we decided to watch the sun set over the river valley while enjoying a cocktail. The light lowered, and a few birds made their final calls of the day from a copse of willows along the creek. An angler came around a bend from downstream. Now just a silhouette in the gloaming, the figure waded slowly, staying low, making deliberate, targeted casts. From our perch, we watched him methodically cover the pool.

"Doesn't he remind you of Dave?" I whispered.

My wife laughed and told me she had been thinking the same thing. We joked that he must have followed us into Yellowstone, and then we toasted to Dave's good health and speedy recovery. The figure waded upstream and disappeared around the next bend.

By now you have probably figured out the end of this story, and yes, it's true. When we returned home, I learned from his wife that Dave had passed away the same day we fished Slough Creek.

The posture and intensity were unmistakable.

DEAD STUFF IN THE WATER

THE IMAGE STILL HAUNTS ME. MIDNIGHT ON A LONELY STRETCH of beach along the bayside of Sandy Hook . . . Dery Bennett and I wading the mouth of the Shrewsbury River casting for striped bass. An autumn nor'easter howled like a wild animal, spitting rain down our slickers. Storm tides had pushed a slick of debris tight against the beach. We waded among floating mats of decaying phragmites peppered with bits of Styrofoam and empty beer cans. Then we saw something bobbing in the tide. At first it looked like a log, or maybe the top of an old piling, but as waves and current swept it closer, it began to transform into something pale and fleshy. When it was practically at our feet, I switched on my headlamp. Two beady eyes stared back lifelessly. A low-slung mouth hung open, circled by thick, ghastly lips. The severed head of an Atlantic sturgeon rolled at the water's edge. Whether it came from a commercial fisherman's net or straight from a shark's mouth didn't matter—it gave us the creeps, that big dead thing. We backed out of the water. Time to go, we both agreed; time to go.

Things die. Bunker get chopped in half by bluefish; stripers chase rainfish onto dry sand, where gulls pick them off by the thousands. Shoals of spawned-out sockeye salmon succumb in Alaskan rivers, with sleek rainbow trout and arctic char scarfing down pieces of their decaying flesh. On trout streams, great mayfly hatches are thinly veiled showcases of death and carnage. Trout slash at hatching insects; dragonflies, swallows, and bats gobble up those that make it off the stream. The mayfly itself expires after it mates and lays its eggs, only to be sucked down by yet another trout once it lands on the water. Some anglers call these spectacles noble and poetic. Others hoot and cheer them on—between casts, of course—like Romans watching slaves getting thrown to the lions.

Similar to the sturgeon's head making its unwanted appearance, sometimes stumbling upon the Grim Reaper's handiwork in nature lacks that certain poetic flair. Once while bushwhacking my way to a good shad fishing spot on the lower Delaware River, I almost ran headlong into a rotting deer carcass dangling from a tree—the by-product of the previous winter's floods. Every time I made a cast, I would glance back only to see those empty eyes, which now seemed to be staring at me. Near this same spot a year later, I flushed a flock of turkey vultures feasting on a bloated piglet that must have drowned before washing downriver from a farm. *Noble* was not a word that came to mind; *repulsive* and *smelly*, on the other hand, seemed to fit nicely.

A few summers ago, I wet-waded a stretch of a suburban river fly fishing for big carp. It started raining, and the river began to swell with runoff from the acres of parking lots and side streets that flush directly into its mildly polluted waters. As I watched the water turn the color of chocolate milk, something soft and hairy brushed my calf. With an uneasy feeling, I looked down, just in time to see a dead muskrat using my legs as a temporary logjam. When I got home, I scrubbed from the waist down with the intensity of a heart surgeon.

Yet, compared to what happened to a friend of mine while trout fishing in upstate New York, I got off easy. He hiked to a small remote stream and, instead of packing a heavy water bottle, decided to bring one of those high-tech osmosis filters in case he got thirsty. He had just finished a long, cold, satisfying drink from the stream before wading upriver to fish the next pool. There he came face to face with the remains of an immense bloated deer slowly spinning round and round in a back eddy. I'm not sure what happened next, but I don't think it involved trout fishing. Mr. Reaper may not always be the sensitive poet, but apparently, he does like a good practical joke now and then.

An Island in Time

Nowadays it's just another sandbar in a New Jersey bay where pleasure boaters and jet skiers haul up in the summer to blast music and drink. At high tide, not much is visible—just a narrow sliver of sand that seems to bob in the low breakers like a corpse.

But it wasn't always this way. More than thirty years ago, in the mid-1990s, I knew it as a remnant coastal island—a small chunk of short dunes, Atlantic cedar trees, bayberry, and beach plum that had separated from the mainland. Oystercatchers would probe the mudflats along the spartina grasses that lined its leeward shore. Gulls loafed among the dunes. Rafts of brant honked and croaked in its coves.

And off the southern point of this diminutive spot was the most bassy looking rip I ever laid eyes on.

There, the ebbing tide would hurry past a cut, churn through a deep hole, and then rise and crash over a bar creating a crescendo of seething, swirling, watery confusion.

It's only appropriate that from this spot, my greatest of all striped bass was taken.

I discovered the rip while on a daytime scouting walk. Through binoculars, I could see it surging with the last of the ebb. I theorized that one could make the two-hundred-yard crossing from the mainland to the little island by wading carefully and avoiding any deep holes or cuts.

I was right; the following night, in a cold drizzle, and under the darkness of the November new moon, my friend Dery and I slowly picked our way through the channel and eventually reached its shores.

We could hear the rip before we saw it—it was the same sound a lively riffle makes on a trout river. When we rounded the south point, we could see it—a dark sinew of rushing water pushed along by spring tides.

Dery, thirty-five years my senior, salty and seasoned, began casting one of his signature ragtag plugs—namely, some old wooden swimmer he likely found washed up on the beach. He ran the American Littoral Society, a coastal conservation group, and I believe he loved the act of fishing far more than actually catching fish. I, on the other hand, the young upstart in my twenties with painstakingly maintained tackle, was out for blood. I opted instead for a live eel—one of a half dozen I had picked up at a tackle shop earlier that evening.

I knelt in the wet sand and took the eel out of a canvas bag before hooking it through its lower jaw. Then I waded into the rip and lobbed it fifty feet uptide, letting it tumble with the current.

The eel drifted maybe ten yards when I felt a solid thump. I let the fish swim with the bait until my arms were fully extended, then I reared back mightily into solid weight. For a moment, nothing happened. Then slowly and unyieldingly, yards and yards of line peeled off the reel as the bass powered farther and farther into the rip, until I thought it would spool all three hundred yards of monofilament. Finally, it stopped and shook its head, sending ponderous thumps up the line, down the rod, through my hands, and into my soul. For some reason, I glanced at my watch, perhaps knowing this would not be a short fight. It was just after midnight.

Meanwhile, Dery had reeled up his plug and enjoyed the show.

For what seemed like a long time, the fish simply held somewhere out there in the rip and sulked. I could almost picture it angled away from me digging into the three-knot current with broad sweeps of its tail.

Minutes passed while I could do little more than hang on, terrified I would lose the big fish. Dery, ever the wise guy, and knowing my deep belief in fishing jinxes, began joking about sharpening up the fillet knife and heading home to light the grill.

"Stop!" I would plead, trying to appease unseen Fishing Gods while stifling back my own laughter.

And so the fight went on. Ten minutes. Fifteen. Twenty-five. Sweat mixed with rainwater trickled down my neck. Hands once cold now felt hot.

Then, a half hour into the fight, I could feel the fish surrender. It moved out of the rip into slack water and began swimming toward me.

I pumped the rod and gobbled up line with each turn of the reel. Before I knew it, I could see a large spiny dorsal fin slice the water twenty feet away. I reeled in more line while wading out deeper to grab the shock leader.

Then, leader in hand, I walked the fish into the shallows. I kept walking until the bay parted, and the most beautiful striped bass I have ever seen slid onto the sand. I looked at my watch again. Thirty-five minutes had passed since I first hooked it.

A quick measurement on my rod would later reveal that the fish was forty-four inches long and perhaps thirty-five pounds. Though it was not the biggest striper I ever landed, it fought the hardest and is still the most perfectly proportioned bass I ever caught, with a smallish head; thick, muscular shoulders; and a deep, round belly.

And despite earlier jokes about a grill and fillet knife, Dery and I both knew we would let it go. I slipped the hook from its softball-sized mouth then posed for a few snapshots from Dery's old camera before I slid the big fish back into the rip. We watched it kick its tail a few times before it vanished into the darkness.

Though it was the only bass taken that night, it marked the beginning of more than a decade of sometimes amazing fishing from this secret and intimate spot.

But over time, the island began to shift and erode. Blame it on climate change, sea level rise, or changing tidal currents, but one by one, the trees toppled into the bay. Then the deep hole filled in and the bar began to shallow out. At the same time, the big stripers—the ones that would prowl the shallows at night—started to vanish from their usual spots. In 2012, two years after Dery died, Superstorm Sandy took care of the rest, flattening it both literally and figuratively.

I still see what's left of the island occasionally on my way to fish somewhere else. Now it's just a sad-looking mound of sand scraped clean of even a blade of dune grass. I try to shrug it off as just another spot that's come and gone, but inevitably memories of the rip, the bass—and, of course, Dery—come rushing in like the November spring tide one rainy night many years ago.

See you on the other side of the river or in the big wash.

ACKNOWLEDGMENTS

VERSIONS OF MANY OF THESE STORIES—SOME SHORTER, SOME longer, some with different titles—first appeared in other publications. For that, I thank the talented, kind, and patient editors who have worked with me over the years: Susan B. Adams from the *New York Times*, Tom Bie from *The Drake*, Gerry Bethge from *Outdoor Life*, Steve Duda from *Patagonia*, Paris Fleezanis from *This Is Fly*, Sam Hudson from *Sport Fishing*, Charlie Levine and Bill Sisson from *Anglers Journal*, Jason Rolfe from the *FlyFish Journal*, Chad Shmukler from *Hatch*, and Greg Thomas from *American Angler*. One of the great thrills for a writer is sending out a story into what can feel like the abyss and then actually hearing back. It's like blind casting a Turk's Tarantula and raising an enormous trout . . . or working a big pencil popper through the breakers for a heavy striper, or . . . wait—what was I saying? Focus. Special thanks to fishing pals Dave Taft, for allowing me access to his sketch book, and Jim Leedom for his photography skills. And to all my other fishing friends, too numerous to mention here but often appearing in my stories, thanks for all the casts.